WITHDRAWN

MODERN MENDING

How to minimize waste and maximize style

ERIN LEWIS-FITZGERALD

Search Press

First published in Great Britain in 2021
Search Press Limited,
Wellwood, North Farm Road,
Tunbridge Wells, Kent TN2 3DR

Originally published by Affirm Press in 2020
This edition is based on the expanded edition published by
Affirm Press in 2021
Copyright © Affirm Press, 28 Thistlethwaite Street, South
Melbourne, Boonwurrung Country, VIC 3205, Australia
www.affirmpress.com.au

Text © Erin Lewis-Fitzgerald 2021
Cover and internal design by Emily Thiang
Photographs by Erin Lewis-Fitzgerald except for pages 182
and 240–252 (supplied by menders)
Illustrations © Claire Robertson 2021

ISBN: 978-1-78221-960-6
ebook ISBN: 978-1-78126-967-1

For my niece Chloe, my nephews Sebastian, Elías, Mateo and Lachlan, and my young friends Eleanor and Lucy; you are the future. This book is my way of teaching you everything I know, even if I can't be there in person.

And for Mom, my first sewing teacher and biggest fan. I love you more!

CONTENTS

FOREWORD

Hello. My name is Hilary Harper, and I'm a mending addict. It's hard to pinpoint the exact moment I got hooked, but I'd wager it was when I peeled back the wrapping paper one Christmas to find my very own tiny, pink plastic sewing machine. I set it up next to Mum's as she whizzed her way through the corduroy dungarees/overalls and velveteen dressing gowns of my childhood, and I came to believe I too could perform this mending magic.

'Magic' doesn't seem too strong a word. As a child, I couldn't believe you could take a pile of fabric and some rick-rack and make a ruched Holly Hobbie dress that five-year-old me would die for. Later, it just seemed normal that clothes, gifts and household goods were created and, when they needed it, mended. Engineering problems were solved, art made, and gigalitres of tea consumed over long afternoons of craft and conversation. I osmosed those skills, and soon I was hooked; I was a mending addict.

Hand sewing was my gateway drug: learning how to judge density and pressure for a needle pushing through fabric; assessing tension and counting stitches when turning heels on socks; and sewing, unpicking, and sewing again to get the seams just right. Back then in the Jurassic era (okay, the 1980s) it was important that mending looked perfect, because repairing your own clothes branded you as poor, or miserly. I can still remember one of my more outrageous cousins telling me she'd once darned a blue woollen skirt with bright orange yarn. She laughed at my shocked giggles.

Oh, how the tables have turned, I hear you say! And it's true: we're seeing more creativity around mending and making, in the circles where menders and makers hang out. But it's still a fairly small and self-contained interest group. That's why we need books like this – books that show how easy mending can be, and how enjoyable. We need images of exciting, creative and beautiful repairs, in bookshops and classrooms, and on workbenches and coffee tables everywhere.

Because – confession time – there are lots of people, like me, who manage to completely forget their early education, and end up doing no sewing at all. In my twenties, I bought all my clothes in charity/thrift shops, and took them in, or let them out, or chopped bits off and sewed them back on in interesting and occasionally functional ways. But when I hit my thirties, and acquired real jobs, something changed. The mending pile kept growing, but there never seemed to be enough time to dive into it. Somehow I'd stopped doing something that actually gave me pleasure and satisfaction... for 20 years. My relationship with Stuff became more easy-come, easy-go, and other things took up my time. It was as if the things I'd used to value had just stopped mattering.

And then came Marge (AKA The Comfiest Top I've Ever Owned).

I first found Marge after baby number 2, when comfort was key. It was roomy and soft, with black and white stripes; when I wore it my husband would ask if I was enjoying my time in the Russian navy. I wore it until the cuffs and collar were frayed almost to extinction, the white stripes were wearing through, and the seams looked like moths had savaged them. It was the melting sea ice of T-shirts, but I couldn't let it go.

Then I met Erin. And I learned that Erin took mending commissions. And lo, Erin beheld the top, and a dazed look came over her face, as if she knew that it would be both a zenith and a nadir in her mending life... The top was christened Large Marge, and it will live on in the annals of visible mending as one of the gnarliest projects ever to be successfully completed by a woman of great vim and dedication (see page 212).

Marge is sassy in her old age now – she even has a tattoo gracing her stripes – and I've decided she'll be like grandfather's axe, with so many new handles and blades that I can't say where she begins and ends.

I also learned that Erin ran mending classes. Reader, I signed up, and that tiny ember inside me started to glow again – partly because Erin's teaching style is so accessible and friendly. And that's what you'll find in this book too – some startlingly easy and interesting techniques, some gorgeous suggestions about colour, and some new-old ideas that will get your fingers itching to riffle through that mending pile.

These days, I'm teaching my own kids how to stitch. My four-year-old was so excited when he sewed a button randomly onto the stomach of his T-shirt that he showed it to everyone at childcare. That's a win, not only because it helps the kids think about consumption differently, but also because it gives them a (literally) material understanding of resources, and creativity, and the lifespan of human preoccupations. But most importantly, it's fun. And if what we do with our clothes can make people feel joy or wonder, or spark a conversation, then that's worth doing.

– Hilary Harper, ABC RN Life Matters *presenter and born-again mender*

INTRODUCTION

I love the art of repair. I will roll up my sleeves and fix just about anything: clothes, shoes, ceramics, household items, bad haircuts and even love lives (I once hosted a singles party at my house called Meet Market to help friends who'd been unlucky in love).

I've been fixing and mending for as long as I can remember, but I haven't always been environmentally aware. I learned to use a sewing machine when I was a kid, so mending was simply the act of remaking the clothes I'd learned to construct. I took those skills for granted for most of my life, assuming that everyone did what I did. It wasn't until 2012, when I started volunteering with community repair organizations and 2014, when I founded the social enterprise Bright Sparks (which repaired electrical appliances), that my eyes really opened to the extent of the waste problem in Australia, my home country and around the world, and I realized just how vital repairs – and repair education – are to a healthy planet.

There is no 'away'

The fashion industry is responsible for around 10% of global greenhouse gas emissions, according to the United Nations Framework Convention on Climate Change (UNFCCC). In her book *Slow Clothing*, Jane Milburn writes that Australians are the world's second-largest consumers of new clothes and textiles (after North Americans), consuming an average 27kg (59lbs 5oz) each year, and disposing of 23kg (50lbs 75oz) of leather and textiles per person each year.

A 2017 YouGov report found that 41% of Australian adults had thrown clothes away in the previous year. More than half cited clothing damage as a reason for tossing clothes. And 30% admitted to throwing away more than 10 items of clothing in the previous year.

Here's a scary thought: when you throw something away, there is no 'away'. Whether you dump unwanted clothing in the rubbish bin or donate it to charity, it still exists – you're just pushing the problem to another location.

When we donate stuff to charity, we only see what we give away – we don't see everyone else's stuff and how much of if there is. The reality is that charity/thrift shops are inundated with fast fashion and can resell only a small portion of what's donated. The rest is usually sent to landfill, shipped offshore or turned into rags. Charity/thrift shops are not going to mend your unwanted clothes for you.

There is another way

A journalist once asked me whether mending could save the planet. Maybe not, I said, but one visibly mended garment might inspire three other people to start mending and become more environmentally aware. Repairing is caring, and awareness and caring are the first steps to tackling the mess we're in. Everyone wears clothes, and just about anyone can mend clothes – including you! – so it's an easy way to start making a difference.

But it's one thing to talk about the problem and what you *should* do, and it's another to have the skills and knowledge to actually do it. Mending is often mentioned as a solution without any practical instructions provided, so you're left to figure it out for yourself. That's where this book comes in.

I wrote *Modern Mending* because the book I wanted did not exist. And the really useful mending books from decades ago are out of print and need updating to suit the clothes we wear now.

I've structured this book in the same way I teach my mending course: with five main techniques, heaps of helpful hints and plenty of examples for inspiration. Think of *Modern Mending* as a cookbook; you don't need to read it from cover to cover and can dip in and out as needed. And think of me as your cheerleader, cheering you on to success. I know you can do it!

Experimend

I use the word *experimend* a few times throughout this book. Damaged textiles are all unique; sometimes you'll need to think outside this book and use your new mendy problem-solving skills to come up with a method, or combination of methods, that works. Some of the tutorials in this book are traditional techniques; others are the result of years of experimending. If you discover a new, better way to mend something, give yourself a pat on the back and share your newfound knowledge with others!

I think it's so important to have a go because that's how you learn. Magic happens when your hands are at work – your hands learn things too, in a different way to looking at a diagram or reading instructions.

Now pop on the kettle and make a cup of tea! I love tea, and I find that the ritual of making it is a lovely (and delicious) way to start a new project, helping you relax, focus and get ready to learn and try new things.

Happy mending!

– Erin Lewis-Fitzgerald

HELPFUL TIPS

1. **The best method is whatever it takes to get the job done!** This is my motto. Sure, some methods will be stronger or more environmentally friendly than others, but it's better to have an imperfectly mended item than an unmended one.

2. When buying mending supplies, **choose colours and materials that make your heart sing** so you're more likely to use them up. If you are someone who likes to take your time selecting colours, fabrics and threads, factor in more time for each technique and make another cup of tea. (For me, this is the fun part!)

3. **Take 'before' photos.** This is a tip from my mom, who lives an ocean away and loves to see 'before' photos of items I've mended. A good before-and-after reveal is always fun and once you start mending, the opportunity for a 'before' photo is lost. Even if you don't show the pictures to anyone, they're good to have for your own learning so you can see how much you've improved.

4. **Join the dots.** I use safety pins to mark all the holes in an item before I start mending it. It helps ensure I mend every single hole (sometimes they're tricky to find when you need to) and identify any potential shapes or designs that might inspire me.

5. **Mend at the first sign of a hole,** or try preventative mending when fabric is threadbare. The longer you wait to mend something and the bigger the holes get, the more work you create for yourself or someone else ($$$) later. If you can't mend something right away, remove it from your wardrobe so it doesn't get worse. And mend before washing, as holes grow larger in the wash (the exception: if someone else is mending a garment for you, the polite thing to do is wash it first).

6. **Match the composition, texture and thickness of your fabric or yarn to the item you're mending,** but experimend with different colours or prints (see This Goes With That, page 28). Sometimes I break this rule; when my sparkle threads (which match nothing) beg me to use them, I cannot resist!

7. **Secure, then embellish.** Stress points need extra reinforcement (e.g. use leather instead of felt on felt slippers if your toes are always pushing through). Patch worn-out buttonholes and ripped belt loops before sewing. Some functional embroidery stitches can do double-duty, but strength should take priority over beauty if something's going to get a lot of wear and be washed often.

8. **You can usually go back and re-mend something later,** once you've had a bit more practice, a flash of inspiration or learned a new technique. Some methods are more permanent than others (see Should I Redo it? page 259) but there's usually an opportunity to improve upon what you started at a later stage.

9. **There will always be more holes,** so why not plan for them? You can choose to be proactive about it, making sure any clothing you acquire is well-made and thinking about how you might mend it when the time comes. See Thoughts Before Mending on the next page for more.

10. **Practise mending on tea towels or scrap fabric first** so you can build up your skills and confidence with nothing to lose. More reasons to love tea towels: 1. they're the most affordable form of art you can have in your home, 2. the sturdy woven fabric makes them easy to stitch for beginners, and 3. they get used often, so you can see how your mends will hold up to regular washing and wear and tear.

THOUGHTS BEFORE MENDING

Before I mend anything, I run through a mental checklist to help me decide how to tackle it.

Here's my usual approach:

1. Come up with too many mending ideas (or some risky ideas) and take months to decide how to proceed.
2. Postpone mending the item for as long as possible, occasionally to the point where it no longer fits me.
3. Finally start mending. Wheee!
4. Decide I hate how it looks and undo my handiwork.
5. Start again with a different method or material. Wheee! Freak out and wonder if this is my Greatest Mend Ever or a Very Bad Idea and I'm ruining my clothes.
6. Finish mending and be genuinely surprised to discover that the mended garment is now my favourite item of clothing ever.
7. Wear it all the time and enjoy the compliments.
8. Repeat as necessary.

Look, I didn't say it was a good approach. But I wanted you to know that I get nervous, too! It's part of the process sometimes and you have to push through to get to the 'favourite thing' stage. But there are some key questions you can ask yourself before you start mending to help you narrow down your options.

Where is the damage and how did it happen?

Was the damage caused by a one-time accident or is it a recurring issue? Sites that get a lot of wear and tear – knees, armpits, crotches, pockets – need extra-strength mending solutions. You could darn knee holes, but patches will be more durable and last longer. If you are the Incredible Hulk and bust out of clothes that are too tight for you in certain areas, sewing them back up is not enough; you'll need a stronger rip solution with reinforcement (or possibly an alteration to give you more room to Hulk freely). Stained or discoloured clothing (without holes or rips) can be revamped with purely decorative, less durable mending methods: fabric dye, fabric paint, embroidery, etc. Personally, I prefer invisible mending for crotches, armpits and other areas where I don't want to attract attention, but visible mending for nearly everywhere else.

What is the item made of?

Is the fabric woven or knit, heavyweight or delicate, made from natural fibres or synthetic? Woolly items are well suited to darning and needle felting, whereas woven items are better candidates for patching.

How will this item be worn and washed?

Tea towels, T-shirts, socks and kids' clothes need durable solutions that can stand up to frequent washing, whereas sweaters should be washed infrequently, by hand or on a delicate wash cycle.

Are the good bits (undamaged sections) of the item strong enough to withstand mending?

Sometimes an item becomes too delicate and threadbare to keep mending, so I make sure the 'good' parts of the item have enough life left in them to be worth saving and to support new stitches and/or material. Clothes that are too far gone can be upcycled into heirloom pieces, such as patchwork quilts, and the best bits from shirts and undies make excellent patches and cleaning rags.

Do the holes form a pattern that could provide inspiration? Is there a design theme or motif that you can replicate?

I like to let the item inspire me. If it has polka dots, I love adding more dots in a different colour. I love contrasting stripes on stripes. If an item features pictures of food, I might add an animal eating it, or if there's a blue background I might add clouds or fish. If something has multiple holes, I'll mark them with safety pins first and step back to see what kind of pattern they establish and what type of design they might inspire. I also consider how the item might look over time – if this is the first (or second) mend, how can I set up my design so future mends will be complementary? And if I'm mending someone else's item, will they be able to easily mend it in future in a way that continues the theme I've started?

What sort of style does the item's owner have?

If I can't decide between a fun or beautiful mending option, I usually ask the owner, and I often consult them on colour choices, too. Kids' clothes might get a more playful mend, and I keep styles and colours to a minimum if mending for my husband. If I'm mending for myself, anything goes, but I usually gravitate toward experimending with a new technique, design or material I haven't tried before – it keeps things interesting for me and means I'm always learning.

PLAYING AROUND WITH A DESIGN

My friend Michael sewed this excellent shirt. He accidentally cut it while he was making it, and his wife, Cindy, mended it with zigzag stitch on the front and a patch on the back.

Michael once asked me how I would have mended it.

This shirt has been mended well, but it's not the only way to mend it. This could be just the starting point, and the rip could be used as inspiration for some fun embellishment.

I've drawn some examples of what I mean, to get you thinking in a different way.

Here you can see the rip up close.

In this example, the rip becomes a patch of grass for frolicking horses.

Or maybe these horses are in LOVE.

Or maybe there's a cowboy with a lasso. (Yee-haw!)

Conversation starter

These examples are slightly silly, and silly is not for everyone. But please put on your activist hat for a moment: bold, funny and interesting mends are more likely to spark people's curiosity and invite questions, which gives you more opportunities to tell the world you've mended what you're wearing. Think of a cute mend as a cute-but-savvy ploy to get people talking about sustainability and slow fashion and all kinds of important, not-cute things we should be discussing more often.

These conversations have two benefits:

1. You encourage people to mend (instead of toss) their clothes, which they might not have considered or thought possible.

2. You challenge preconceived notions about what mending looks like, showing people that it can be fun and/or beautiful.

These conversations don't have to happen in person – they can be online, too.

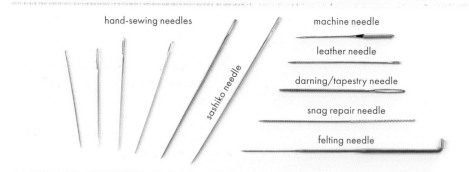

hand-sewing needles

machine needle

leather needle

darning/tapestry needle

sashiko needle

snag repair needle

felting needle

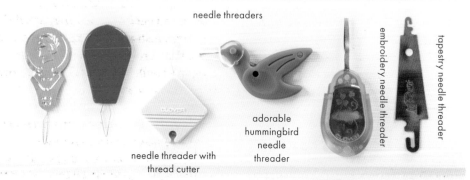

needle threaders

needle threader with
thread cutter

adorable
hummingbird
needle
threader

embroidery needle threader

tapestry needle threader

jar for safe collection of broken/bent/dull pins and needles

TOOLS OF THE TRADE

This section lists the tools and materials you'll need for each technique.

Don't let the number of items on these pages scare you. They're not all necessary but some can provide extra help if you need it.

NEEDLES

Hand-sewing needles are essential in any mending toolkit. As a rule of thumb, choose the thinnest needle with an eye large enough to accommodate your chosen thread. Thin needles are best for thin, delicate fabrics, like silk and cotton voile, to avoid damaging them, and thicker needles are better for sturdy threads and fabrics (e.g. denim). I use a few types:

o   Sharps are general hand-sewing needles with small eyes.
o   I use long embroidery needles with large eyes for most mending jobs.
o   Darning or tapestry needles are perfect for darning hand-knit garments. They have a large eye to fit thick yarn and a blunt tip that prevents yarn from splitting.
o   Extra-long sashiko needles are perfect for sashiko stitching.
o   Leather needles are useful for stitching leather and other heavy-duty materials (I've used them to stitch plastic and wetsuit fabric).

Sewing-machine needles come in different sizes and types. You can buy universal needles for general use or choose a pack specific to what you're sewing – jersey/knits needles for T-shirts, delicate needles for delicate fabrics like silk, chiffon and cotton voile, and denim or heavy-duty needles for denim and canvas.

Felting needles have tiny notches that bond fibres together.

Snag repair needles are a huge time-saver if you need to repair snags in fabric regularly. Instead of an eye, a snag repair needle has a rough surface that grabs snags and pulls them down through your fabric to the other side.

Needle threaders are a savvy invention and there's no shame in using one! Especially if it makes you more efficient and less anxious about mending. I like specialty needle threaders for tapestry and embroidery; they're more durable than wire threaders (which tend to break easily) and are better suited to the thick threads I use a lot.

Needle collection jars are the safest solution for storing broken needles that are too small and sharp to be safely recycled or binned on their own. I collect my broken, bent and dull needles and pins in an old spice jar, then empty it into a sharps container for safe disposal.

CLOTHES IRON

Your iron is your friend!
○ It removes wrinkles from fabric.
○ It attaches patches (with fusible web).
○ It gives your repairs a polished look.
○ It makes your mending less visible if you're aiming for a blended mend.

For best results, use the recommended heat setting for the most delicate part of the item you've mended. Embroidery looks best when it's ironed from the wrong side. And steam is the secret to smoothing out needle felting, darning, snags and ladder repairs. But turn off the steam when you're making patches so you don't burn your fingers.

THIMBLES

A thimble protects your finger and provides a hard surface that's handy for pushing your needle through thick fabric. Thimbles come in many styles and sizes; it's worth trying them out to find one you like that fits comfortably on your preferred finger. My favourite is a soft leather thimble (pictured on my index finger); you can make your own from scrap leather.

PINS & SAFETY PINS

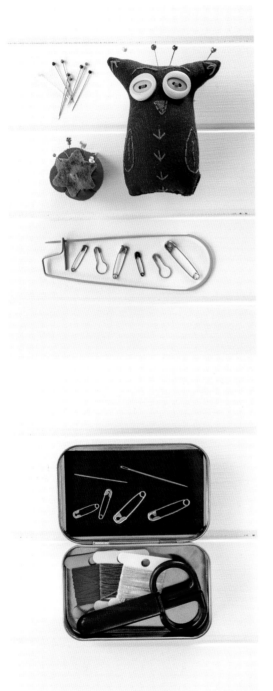

Pins are useful for temporarily attaching patch fabric to the item you're mending, to hold it securely in place while you stitch. I like glass-head pins because you can iron over them and they won't melt. And for hand stitching, I prefer safety pins because I'm less likely to get stuck by accident.

TRAVEL KIT

My travel mending kit is an old mint tin with a fridge magnet stuck in the lid to hold needles and safety pins. It contains a small pair of scissors with a protective cap so the sharp tips won't destroy my stuff while I'm on the go. (If your scissors don't have a protective cap or sheath, you can hand sew one from scrap leather.)

If you're planning to mend on an aeroplane, it's best to check current airline regulations to find out which tools are allowed – the rules change regularly and can differ depending on your airline and destination.

Fabric-marking tools are handy for drawing stitch lines, outlines, and cut lines. It's best to test them on an inconspicuous part of your garment first (e.g. an inside seam), as they can be difficult to remove from certain fabrics. Remove any marks before you iron, as heat could set them permanently.

Micron pens (left) are permanent but great for tracing embroidery patterns and lettering when you want a fine line.

Hera markers (second from left) make temporary creases that disappear in the wash.

Chalk (middle) is sold as tailor's chalk (a solid piece), chalk pencils, powdered chalk liners and transfer paper. Sweat and repeated rubbing can make chalk lines disappear, so I prefer not to use it for complex stitching projects.

Air-erasable fabric markers (third from right) contain ink that disappears over time, so are risky for long-term projects.

Water-erasable fabric markers (second from right and far right) are my favourite marking tools. Crayola washable markers (removable with soapy water) are a clever option and come in many colours.

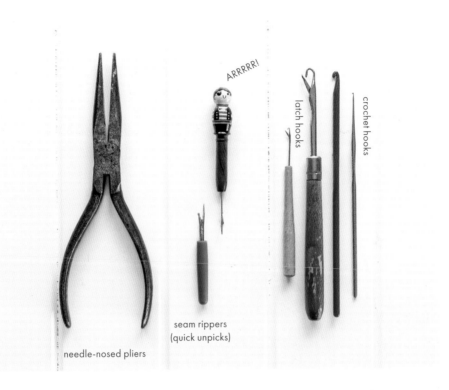

ARRRRR!

latch hooks

crochet hooks

seam rippers
(quick unpicks)

needle-nosed pliers

Needle-nosed pliers can help you pull your needle through thick material when a thimble isn't enough – useful for tough mending jobs like jeans and shoes. They're also helpful for some zipper repairs.

Seam rippers, or quick unpicks, are great for unpicking seams when you need better access to the area you're mending. They are also useful for removing stitching mistakes but use a light touch, as it's possible to damage an item and poke more holes in it if you're not careful. I tend to use a seam ripper to remove machine stitching and small, sharp scissors to remove hand stitches.

Crochet hooks and latch hooks are handy for fixing ladders (dropped stitches) in knitwear (see page 162 to learn how). Crochet hooks come in many sizes and are easy to find new and second-hand. Ladder darners (latch hooks) were used for this task when mending was common; the latch keeps your yarn from falling off the hook while you pull it through. But they're harder to find now; search online for micro latch hooks, usually sold as hair-weaving tools.

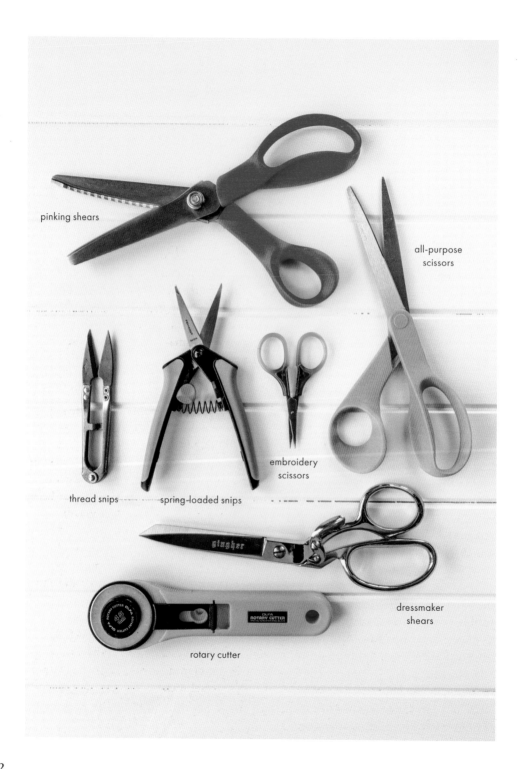

pinking shears

all-purpose
scissors

thread snips

spring-loaded snips

embroidery
scissors

dressmaker
shears

rotary cutter

22

SCISSORS

Sharp, well-made scissors make mending easier and more enjoyable. You only need one good pair in your mending kit, but I use a few for different purposes.

Note: keep a separate pair of scissors just for cutting fabrics and threads, as paper can dull scissor blades.

Embroidery scissors are great for detailed work, e.g. snipping threads, removing stitches, cutting sections of lace for patching, or trimming fuzzy fibres from a finished needle-felted mend. If I could have only one pair of scissors, I'd choose these. You don't need specialty embroidery scissors, though – any small scissors with sharp points (such as nail scissors) will do.

All-purpose scissors are fine for most mending jobs. I have a pair for cutting fusible web and other sticky materials, as adhesives can dull the blades of good sewing scissors.

Thread snips do just what the name suggests. I always keep a pair by my sewing machine.

Spring-loaded snips are a good option when traditional scissors are uncomfortable or difficult to use. They're great for cutting holes in fabric (if you want to practise mending) and for reverse appliqué. Because the blades are sharp and small, they can be used for embroidery as well.

Pinking shears create a zigzag edge that prevents fabric from fraying – a low-tech alternative to using an overlocker/serger or sewing machine to finish seams. They can make DIY iron-on patches a bit more special, too. Again, don't use these to cut paper, as it will dull the blades and they're difficult to sharpen.

Dressmaker shears cut through heavyweight fabrics, such as denim and canvas, like butter!

Rotary cutters are useful for cutting straight edges on patches. You can roll the blade along the edge of a ruler (with a self-healing mat underneath).

STABILITY AIDS

Embroidery hoops keep fabric smooth and taut – perfect for stitching and darning on woven (non-stretch) fabric but less useful for knit fabric (try using fabric stabilizer instead). Ideally the hoop should be larger than the area you're mending; 15cm (6in) is a good average size. When mending a full-blown hole or rip, be careful not to overstretch your fabric in the hoop or your stitching/darning will become floppy and distorted once the hoop is removed. (Check that the warp and weft threads are in alignment – see Fabric 101 on next page – and not wavy around the hole.) If you're darning a large hole or rip, paper might be a better option.

Darning mushrooms are useful for darning curved items like socks, and the handles can be used to darn glove fingers. Darning mushrooms used to be common but are harder to find now; search online for vintage darning mushrooms or use...

Oranges! Oranges and other citrus can do the same job as darning mushrooms, with three added bonuses: they're easy to acquire, when you poke them with a needle they release a lovely fragrance, and you can eat them afterwards. Mandarins are a good size for kids' socks; for bonus enviro-points teach the kids in your life to darn their own socks!

Paper can be used as a flat stabilizer for darning projects where an embroidery hoop or darning mushroom might warp or stretch the fabric too much. Place a sheet of paper underneath the area to be mended and tack/baste it in place along the edges with sewing thread (see Tacking/basting, page 48). Darn the garment (but not the paper), then remove the tacking/basting stitches and paper when you're finished.

Fabric stabilizers makes stretch fabrics easier to work with; you can find them in major craft shops. Tack/baste or pin the stabilizer in place, stitch through the fabric and stabilizer together, then rinse or tear away the excess when you're finished. Water-soluble stabilizer is easier to use and can be sheer or clear, so you can trace a design and place it on top of your work with a view of the damaged area underneath. But I haven't found a truly environmentally friendly version yet, so use it sparingly and don't waste it. Cotton tearaway stabilizer is more environmentally friendly, but it's opaque so it's best used underneath your work.

Beeswax and thread conditioner coat your thread to prevent tangles, knots and swear words. If you're stitching with old, low-quality or particularly tangly thread, waxing can help make it more workable. For a vegan alternative try a bar of soap.

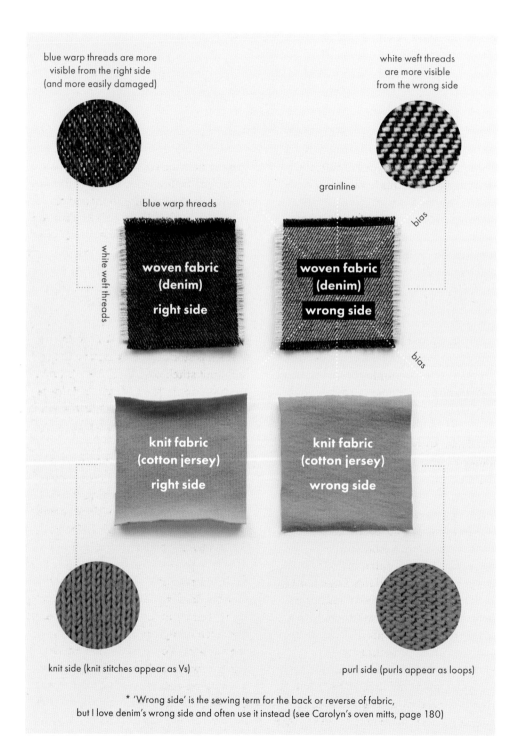

blue warp threads are more
visible from the right side
(and more easily damaged)

white weft threads
are more visible
from the wrong side

blue warp threads

grainline

bias

white weft threads

**woven fabric
(denim)**

right side

**woven fabric
(denim)**

wrong side

bias

**knit fabric
(cotton jersey)**

right side

**knit fabric
(cotton jersey)**

wrong side

knit side (knit stitches appear as Vs)

purl side (purls appear as loops)

* 'Wrong side' is the sewing term for the back or reverse of fabric,
but I love denim's wrong side and often use it instead (see Carolyn's oven mitts, page 180)

FABRIC 101

There are two main types of fabric that I mention in this book: woven and knit fabric.

Woven fabric is created by weaving weft threads (running left to right, or 'weft to wight' for an easy way to remember it) through warp threads (running top to bottom). It is not usually stretchy unless synthetic fibres (such as elastane) have been added.

A woven fabric's grainline is an imaginary vertical line that follows the warp threads, and its bias is diagonal (in either direction). A fabric's bias is stretchier, so avoid pulling or stitching along it – unless more stretch is what you want.

For best results, align your darning and the grainline of your patch fabric with the grainline of the fabric you're mending. When framing fabric in an embroidery hoop, pull the fabric taut in the direction of the warp (grainline or straight grain) and weft, not the bias (the diagonal of the fabric), or your fabric could distort unintentionally.

Denim is a type of fabric known as twill; its weave pattern looks like diagonal ridges, which is more noticeable on paler denim and from the inside of your jeans. For well-blended machine darning, stitch with the grainline or diagonal ridges of your fabric – whichever is more noticeable. For stretch jeans, stitching and darning on the bias will give you more movement.

Knit fabric is created by knitting thread or yarn together in interconnected loops. The most common knit-stitch pattern is stocking/stockinette stitch, with knit stitches that look like Vs on the front and purls that look like little loops or waves on the back. This knit pattern is what gives the fabric its stretch.

A knit fabric's grainline follows the vertical columns of Vs or loops known as wales. For best results, align your darning and the grainline of your patch fabric with the grainline of the fabric you're mending.

If you darn knit fabric using the classic (woven) darning method, the darn won't be as stretchy as the item you're mending. If stretch is important, weave your second pass of darning stitches on the bias or choose a Swiss darn, Scotch darn or stocking-web darn stitch instead (see pages 107–115).

THIS GOES WITH THAT

In Helpful Hints, I share this tip: 'match the composition, texture and thickness of your fabric or yarn to the item you're mending'. If you're not familiar with fabric or yarn, that tip might sound daunting. So I've created this visual guide, matching common fabrics you might need to mend with the materials, needles and techniques best suited to mending them.

When I say composition I mean the fibres that make up the fabric: cotton, wool, leather, silk, etc. Matching fibre types means the item you're mending can be washed in the same way as the materials used to mend it, and you won't be surprised by differences in shrinkage. (When making patches from new fabric, prewashing is recommended.)

Texture refers to the fabric's look and feel. Is it fuzzy? Shiny? Delicate and sheer? A good texture match makes a mend look more seamless and intentional.

For thickness the aim is to avoid extremes:
o   Heavy fabric can weigh down lightweight fabric, making it more prone to ripping.
o   Yarn that's too thick can look lumpy and feel uncomfortable in a darned sock.
o   If you darn with yarn that's too thin, you could darn for days (or not close the hole).
o   A stretchy item patched with stiff fabric might not fit or function the same way.

This is not a complete list, and you are free to experiment! To quote Picasso: 'Learn the rules like a pro, so you can break them like an artist.'

cotton darning needle

universal machine needle

lightweight cotton

all-purpose sewing thread

topstitching thread

embroidery thread/floss

fine hand-sewing needle (sharp)

universal machine needle

WOVEN COTTON

Stitch with: all-purpose sewing thread, topstitching thread, embroidery thread/floss, sashiko thread

Patch with: cotton and cotton blends of similar thickness, linen

Darn with: embroidery thread/floss (1-3 strands), cotton mending yarn

Machine darn with: all-purpose sewing thread

Suitable needles: hand-sewing needles, cotton darning needles, embroidery needles, universal machine needles (sizes 70/10 – 90/14, depending on thickness)

Woven cotton is commonly found in shirts, trousers, dresses and household linens. Patch extra-thin garments with extra-thin cotton to avoid weighing down the fabric and causing further damage, and use a fine needle. Lightweight woven cottons – quilting cotton, shirting, chambray and flannel – are more versatile, both as mending subjects and as patch fabrics.

Patch extra-thin cotton with cotton voile, cotton lawn or old sheets (grey voile used for Emily O's shirt, page 194)

COTTON JERSEY

Stitch with: all-purpose sewing thread, embroidery thread/floss (1-2 strands)

Patch with: cotton or cotton-blend jersey, cotton interlock

Darn with: embroidery thread/floss (1-3 strands for most jersey), cotton mending yarn, tapestry cotton (for thick socks)

Suitable needles: hand-sewing needles (ballpoint or sharps), embroidery needles, cotton darning needles, jersey or ballpoint machine needles (size 80/12)

Cotton jersey (including cotton blends) is a soft, stretchy fabric commonly found in T-shirts, underwear, socks and leggings. It can be challenging to mend because it curls and stretches, but it doesn't fray so it's great for raw-edge patches. Water-soluble stabilizer or fusible web can be used to stabilize jersey before you stitch, or a darning mushroom before you darn.

all-purpose sewing thread

embroidery thread/floss

hand-sewing needle

machine needle
(jersey or ballpoint)

cotton interlock
(used for Large Marge,
page 212)

cotton jersey
(used for Large Marge, page 212)

all-purpose sewing thread

topstitching thread

sashiko thread

hand-sewing needle

sashiko needle

old jeans
(used for Emma M's jeans, page 202)

cotton canvas

DENIM

Stitch with: all-purpose sewing thread, topstitching thread, sashiko thread, embroidery thread/floss

Patch with: denim, canvas, cotton duck

Darn with: embroidery thread/floss, cotton mending yarn

Machine darn with: all-purpose sewing thread and thin cotton fabric

Suitable needles: strong hand-sewing needles, embroidery needles, sashiko needles, cotton darning needles, jeans/denim or universal machine needles (size 90/14 or 100/16)

Denim is a heavy woven twill fabric found in jeans and jackets. Originally made from 100% cotton, it's now often combined with synthetic fibres to give it stretch and body-hugging properties. For best results patch denim with denim of similar thickness and stretchiness – e.g. raw 100% cotton denim with raw 100% cotton denim, and thin stretch denim with thin stretch denim. The exception is machine darning – the extra stitching adds bulk, so thin, soft fabrics are the best patch choice when machine darning.

denim machine needle

Thin cotton (recommended for machine darning only)

various linen threads

all-purpose sewing thread

topstitching thread

embroidery thread/floss

hand-sewing needle

universal machine needle

linen

LINEN

Stitch with: all-purpose sewing thread, linen thread, embroidery thread/floss, sashiko thread

Patch with: linen, hemp, cotton, canvas (for thick linen)

Darn with: embroidery thread/floss, linen thread, cotton mending yarn

Machine darn with: all-purpose sewing thread

Suitable needles: hand-sewing needles (sharps), embroidery needles, sashiko needles, cotton darning needles, universal machine needles (size 80/12 or 90/14)

Linen is a strong, long-lasting fabric made from flax fibres, most commonly seen in shirts, trousers, dresses and household linens (hence the name!). It wrinkles and frays easily but wears well over time and provides a good variety of mending options. Linen is usually woven but can be made into knitwear; linen knits are prone to damage and not as long-lasting but can still be mended by darning or patching with other lightweight fabrics such as lace.

cotton

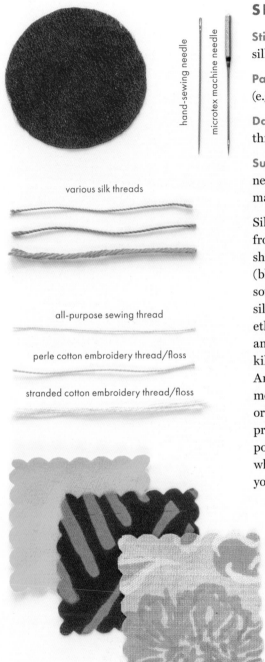

various silk threads

all-purpose sewing thread

perle cotton embroidery thread/floss

stranded cotton embroidery thread/floss

hand-sewing needle

microtex machine needle

SILK

Stitch with: all-purpose sewing thread, silk thread, embroidery thread/floss

Patch with: silk, silk-like fabrics (e.g. some rayon and polyester)

Darn with: silk thread, embroidery thread/floss (1-2 strands)

Suitable needles: fine hand-sewing needles (sharps), microtex or universal machine needles (size 70/10 or 80/11)

Silk is a premium woven fabric made from silkworm cocoons, found in shirts, dresses and sometimes knitwear (blended with other fibres). It can be soft, slippery and lustrous or – with raw silk – have a rough, rustic texture. Silk is ethically complex: the fibres are natural and compostable, but silkworms are killed in the process of making them. An ethical, eco-friendly option is to mend silk with second-hand silk fabric or thread, or to use fabric with similar properties (polyester, cotton, etc.). It is possible to unintentionally damage silk when sewing it, so use the finest needles you have to avoid further damage.

silk

silk-like synthetic fabric

aran/worsted wool knitting yarn
used to knit orange circle

wool yarn of similar thickness

4-ply tapestry wool

large darning needle with blunt point

chunky wool yarn used to knit red circle

wool yarn of similar thickness

multiple stands of tapestry wool

BIG KNITS

Stitch/darn with: knitting yarn made
from similar fibres (e.g. wool or cotton),
tapestry wool

Patch with: felt, leather

Suitable needles: large darning or
tapestry needles with blunt points

Big knits – fabrics knitted by hand from
thick yarn – are commonly seen in the
form of sweaters, hats, scarves and socks.
Knitting yarn is best for darning big
knits. If you need help finding a suitable
match, visit your local yarn shop or ask
a knitter friend for advice (and yarn
scraps!). You can combine lengths of thin
yarn to make up the correct thickness,
but the reverse doesn't always hold true;
some yarns can be separated into thinner
strands (plies) successfully, but others
need all of their plies to hold together.
Needle felting is not recommended for
big knits mainly for aesthetic reasons, as
the texture is quite different. Try darning
big knits instead.

Scrap leather or wool felt (from shrunken sweaters
or old blankets) can be used to make elbow patches

34

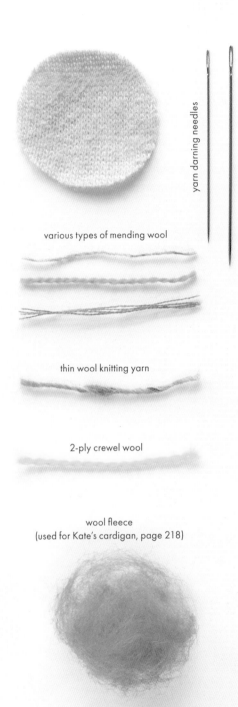

various types of mending wool

thin wool knitting yarn

2-ply crewel wool

wool fleece
(used for Kate's cardigan, page 218)

yarn darning needles

felting needle

FINE KNITS

Stitch with: mending wool, crewel wool, embroidery thread/floss

Darn with: fine knitting yarn made from similar fibres (e.g. wool or cotton), crewel wool, mending wool

Needle felt with: wool fleece

Patch with: fine knits, felt, leather

Suitable needles: hand-sewing needles with large eyes, yarn darning needles, felting needles

Fine knits – fabrics knitted or woven by machine with fine yarn, usually made of wool, cashmere or other animal fibres – are commonly found in the form of sweaters, hats, scarves, socks and thermal base layers. Fine knits are prized for their softness and layering abilities. The woolly variety is delicious to moths but also versatile when it comes to mending options, giving you many creative possibilities.

Fine knits, scrap leather or wool felt can be used to make elbow patches

35

leather hand-sewing needle

leather machine needle

linen thread

heavy-duty thread

topstitching thread

LEATHER

Stitch with: heavy-duty thread, topstitching thread, waxed linen thread

Patch with: leather, suede, faux leather (vinyl or polyurethane)

Suitable needles: leather hand-sewing needles, leather machine needles

Leather, made from animal hides, is commonly found in shoes, jackets, bags, belts and furniture. It can be smooth or textured, in the case of suede. Leather is ethically complex: it's natural, strong and more durable than vinyl (which tends to flake over time), but animals are killed in the process of making it. An ethical, eco-friendly option is to choose second-hand leather goods, maintain them well, and/or mend them with second-hand leather scraps (from old leather goods beyond repair, or ask shoe repairers for scraps). Leather needles are indispensable for sewing leather. They make permanent holes, though, so plan your stitches in advance.

leather
(used to patch Leta's dress no. 2, page 228)

suede

faux leather (vinyl)

hand-sewing needle

universal machine needle

all-purpose sewing thread (polyester)

ballpoint machine needle (for stretch fabrics)

SYNTHETIC FABRICS

Stitch with: all-purpose sewing thread (polyester)

Patch with: synthetic fabrics of similar thickness, texture and stretchiness

Suitable needles: hand-sewing needles (sharps for wovens, ballpoints for knits), universal machine needles for woven fabrics or ballpoint machine needles for stretch fabrics

Synthetic fabrics – polyester, nylon, acrylic, elastane (such as Spandex and Lycra) – are woven from petroleum-based fibres (i.e. plastic), making them affordable in the short term but bad for the planet in the long term. They're commonly found in activewear, outerwear, office attire and... well... everything nowadays (estimates range from 60–75% of all new clothing). There are many types but it's not always easy to identify them, so here are some general guidelines for mending with synthetic fabrics:

For fabric blends with less than 50% synthetic content, follow the recommendations for the main fabric type shown on the previous pages.

For mostly synthetic fabrics:
o Stitch with polyester thread (or a poly-blend).
o If it's stretchy, mend with fabric of similar stretchiness and thickness, and use a stretchy stitch and ballpoint needle for best results.
o If it's sheer and delicate, mend with similarly sheer and delicate fabric and a fine needle. ×

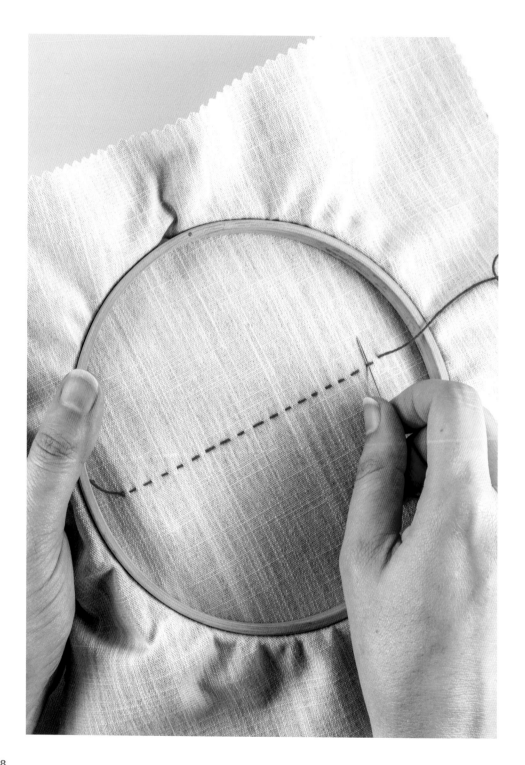

TECHNIQUE:

stitching

Hand stitching is such a valuable, versatile skill; you can stitch in a practical way to mend or reinforce fabric, and you can embellish your mends to make them extra-special.

Hand stitching can be the quickest method for small jobs, like reattaching a button or fixing a hem that's come undone, and it can be slow, repetitive work for larger mends. But this slow, repetitive quality can be a great thing, helping you get into the flow and achieve a more relaxed state of mind.

The tools for hand stitching are simple and portable, so it's a great way to pass the time while travelling or sitting in a waiting room.

In this section, I've included my favourite hand stitches for visible and invisible mending, used by menders, embroiderers and tailors. This is a small selection of all the stitches that exist; check out Recommended Reading (page 264) for more inspiration.

There's no one correct way to stitch fabric – my motto is 'whatever it takes to get the job done'. It doesn't matter whether you stitch up, down, left or right, or how you hold the needle, as long as you get there in the end and the item you're mending is less broken than when you started.

Aim for a consistent stitch length and even tension when you stitch, not perfection; you are a human, not a sewing machine. My students practise their stitching on cotton tea towels – smooth, sturdy fabric is helpful for beginners, and striped tea towels have built-in stitch lines for you to follow.

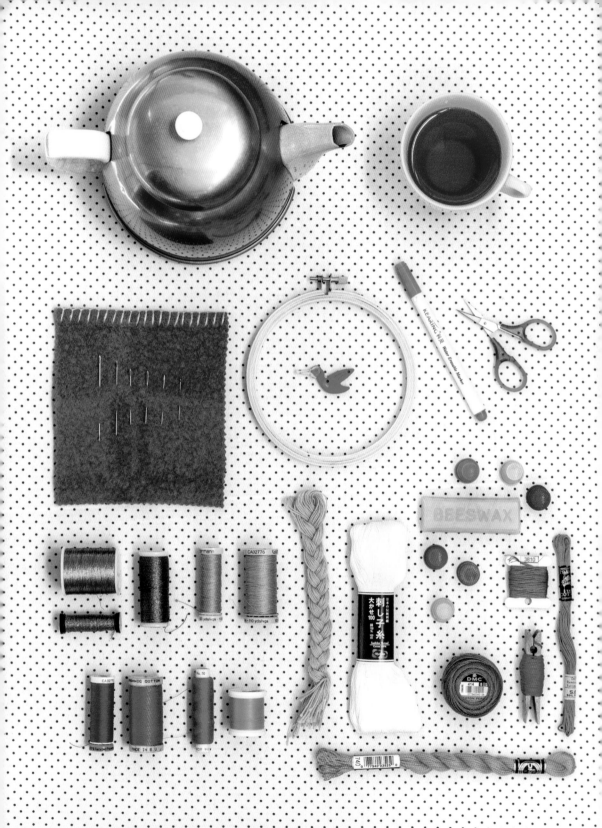

WHAT YOU NEED

THE ESSENTIALS

Fabric that needs a bit of TLC. Stitching is easiest on non-stretchy fabrics, but you can stitch knits and stretch fabrics, too – use fabric stabilizer or just take extra care not to stretch the fabric while you stitch.

Thread to stitch with. Use matching-colour thread for a blended mend or a different colour for visible mending.

o All-purpose sewing thread is made from polyester, cotton or a mixture. It's inexpensive and easy to find.
o Heavy-duty thread/upholstery thread is useful for hand sewing buttons and repairing leather and outdoor gear.
o Topstitching thread is extra-thick and useful for replicating machine-sewn topstitching (e.g. jean hems) and for hand sewing buttons and buttonholes.
o Stranded cotton embroidery thread/floss has 6 strands; you choose how many to use at a time. To avoid tangles, wrap embroidery thread/floss around bobbins or clothes pegs/pins (pictured) before you use it.
o Perle cotton embroidery thread/floss is twisted like rope and not meant to be separated. It adds a lovely texture.
o Sashiko thread is Japanese cotton thread perfect for mending denim. To avoid tangles, cut and plait

sashiko thread (pictured) before you use it.
o Sparkly thread is fun for visible mending.
o Human hair (yes, really!) can be used for mending.

A hand-sewing needle to suit your thread and fabric. See Tools of the Trade (page 16) for details.

A sharp pair of scissors for snipping threads and removing unwanted stitches.

OPTIONAL EXTRAS

These items can make stitching easier; see Tools of the Trade for details.

Beeswax or thread conditioner to prevent tangles, knots and swear words.

A needle threader to make threading your needle easier.

A thimble or needle-nosed pliers for stitching through thick fabric layers.

Pins or safety pins for holding hems and seams together while you stitch.

An embroidery hoop to keep fabric taut.

A fabric-marking tool for drawing stitch lines before you mend.

Fabric stabilizer for stretch fabric.

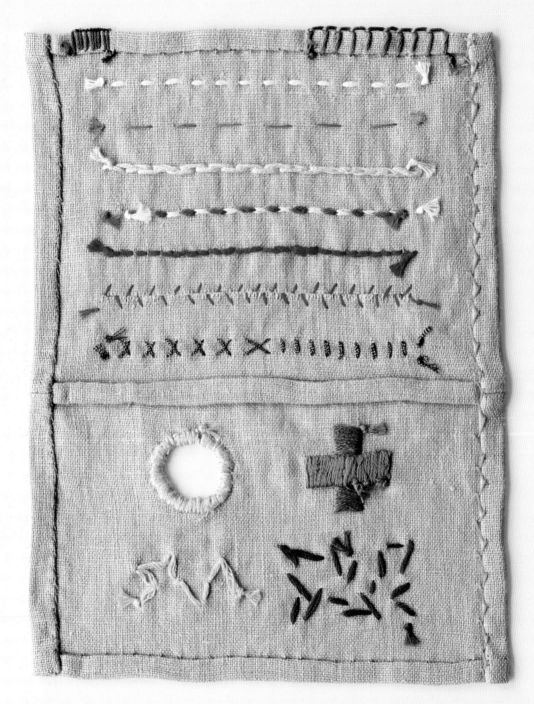

BACK

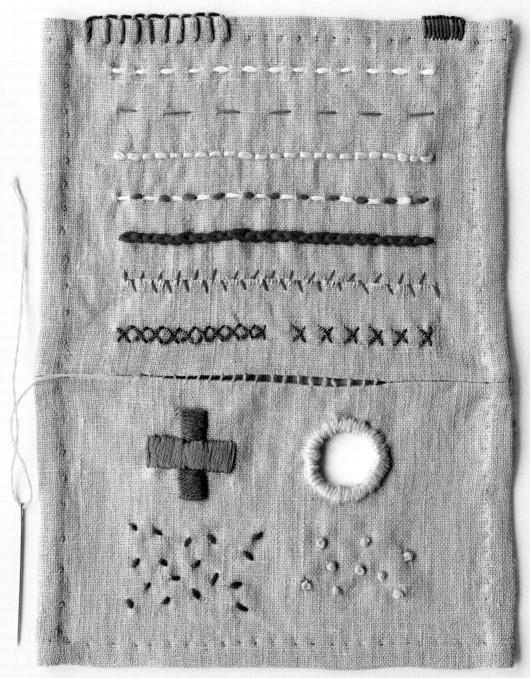

FRONT

1. It's tea time! Make a cup of tea for a quick fix or a pot (or travel mug) if it's a bigger project.

2. Optional: frame your fabric in an embroidery hoop.

    a. Unscrew the hoop to loosen it without removing the screw.

    b. Remove the outer hoop and place your fabric over the inner hoop, with the area to be stitched in the centre.

    c. Replace the outer hoop over the top of the fabric (you might need to unscrew it further to make it fit). Tighten the screw until the fabric is secure.

    d. Pull the fabric taut but not too tight along the warp and weft threads (see Fabric 101 on page 26 for details). When mending a full-blown hole or a rip, be careful not to overstretch your fabric in the hoop or your stitching will become distorted once the hoop is removed. You can use the warp and weft threads of your fabric as a guide to make sure everything's lined up properly.

3. If you're sewing trousers or sleeves, place a book or a piece of stiff cardboard inside to separate the fabric layers and keep you from sewing them shut.

4

6

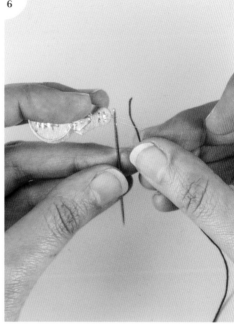

4. Cut your thread. The ideal thread length for stitching is the length of your forearm, from your fingertips to your elbow. Thread can get twisted, tangled and knotty the more you work with it; this length minimizes tangles and ensures you can pull the thread all the way through your fabric in one motion. Cutting your thread at an angle can help make threading the needle easier, too.

5. Optional: drag your thread over a bar of beeswax to make it easier to work with and prevent tangles.

6. Thread your needle, directly or with a needle threader (pictured). Other tricks I use: licking the thread end, moving the needle toward the thread (not vice versa), and folding thread back on itself to make a nice edge.

7. Decide whether to stitch with a single or double length of thread. (I double my thread for buttons or heavy-duty mending.) Then tie a knot at the end; my favourite is the quilter's knot (next page).

8. Get stitching! Follow the stitching methods on pages 48–53.

METHOD: QUILTER'S KNOT

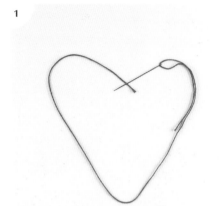

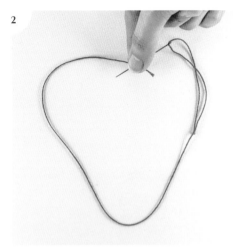

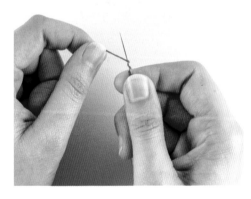

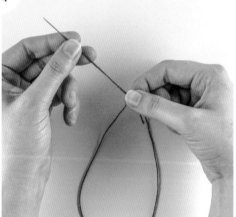

This is a strong and secure knot. Once you get the hang of it, you will love it!

1. Make a loop with your needle and thread pointed in opposite directions.

2. Pinch the needle and thread together with your thumb and index finger.

3. With your opposite hand, tightly coil the thread around your needle at least twice – more for a larger knot.

4. Slip the coiled thread under your pinched thumb and finger. While holding the needle with your other hand, slide the coil all the way down the length of the thread.

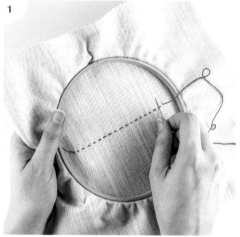

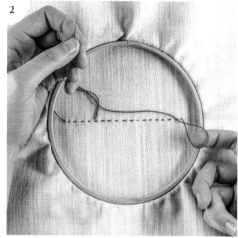

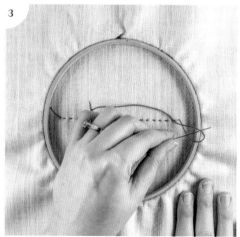

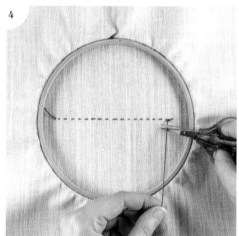

For this method, you'll need to leave enough thread at the end – about double the length of your needle.

1. On the wrong side of the fabric, weave your needle and thread under the last stitch you've made (as shown), or through a thread or two of nearby fabric.

2. Pull through to form a small loop, then give it a twist.

3. Move your needle through the twisted loop and make a knot at the base of the fabric. Repeat as necessary for added strength.

4. Trim the excess thread, leaving a few millimetres (⅛in) beyond the knot.

STITCH METHODS

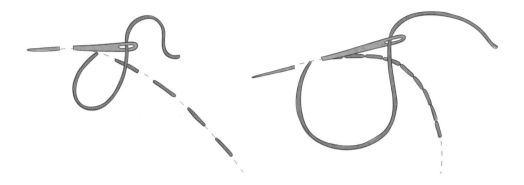

RUNNING STITCH

Running stitch is useful for repairing busted seams, sewing patch edges, and for quilting together layers of fabric to make them stronger. Running stitches are usually the same length as the gaps between them, or slightly longer than the gaps.

I like to load my needle with a few stitches at a time before I pull it and thread through the fabric – it saves time and produces a straighter line. (Long sashiko and embroidery needles are designed for picking up multiple stitches at a time.)

TACKING/BASTING

Tacking/basting is a way to hold layers of fabric together temporarily, with stitches instead of pins or glue. It's essentially running stitch but with much longer stitches, and knots aren't required because the stitches are temporary and will be removed later.

BACKSTITCH

Backstitch is my favourite and the stitching equivalent of 'two steps forward, one step back'. It looks beautiful on top but messy underneath, so it's best for clothes and linens where the underside won't be visible.

As a mending stitch, it's useful for seams, for replicating the look of machine stitching (when using a sewing machine isn't practical), and as an edge stitch for patches. It's strong and flexible and a good choice for mending T-shirts. As a decorative stitch, it's great for lettering, for making faces and for turning stains into features.

There are a few variations of backstitch, but for the classic method there should be no gaps between stitches; your needle should enter the fabric at the same hole created by the previous stitch (or as close to it as possible).

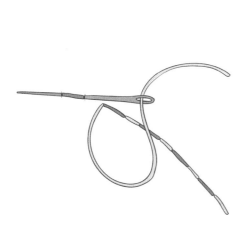

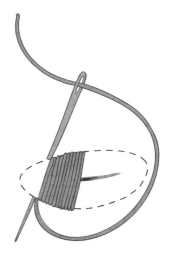

DOUBLE RUNNING STITCH

Double running stitch is a clever alternative to backstitch when you need both sides of your stitching to look neat and using a sewing machine is not practical. Start with a line of running stitch, then make a second pass of running stitches in the opposite direction to fill in the gaps, using the original holes as your guide. Double running stitch looks the same on both sides but does not tend to create as straight a line as backstitch or machine stitching. For a blended mend, use the same thread for both passes, or a different colour for each pass (pictured) for a more playful look.

SATIN STITCH

Satin stitch is an embroidery stitch with a secret super power: mending small holes and rips that are 1cm (⅜in) or less in width. You can also use it to cover up stains in a decorative way.

Draw an outline of your shape first to use as a guide; the damage should be inside the outline with a margin of at least a few millimetres (⅛in). If desired, backstitch along the outline first to help make a neater shape.

Make your satin stitches close together, and bring your needle up on the same side and down on the opposite side of the shape every time. For long shapes, stitch across the thinnest part; long stitches are more likely to become loose and sloppy in the wash.

Satin stitch can be challenging for beginners; it's a good one to practise first. Circles are more challenging; for best results begin stitching in the centre and work your way out.

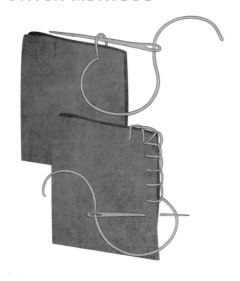

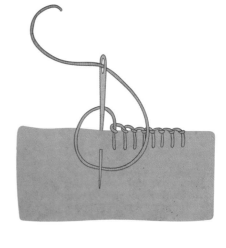

BLANKET STITCH

Blanket stitch is great for mending and reinforcing the edges of blankets and sweaters, and it's a common edge stitch for patches. Start blanket stitch by making a tight loop: wrap your thread around the fabric edge and re-enter through the same hole with your needle, then pass your needle through the loop as shown. Now you can start the blanket-stitch pattern a few millimetres (⅛in) to the side of your first loop, weaving the needle down and out of your fabric in a single step, as illustrated, to catch the thread and secure it. For best results aim for a consistent stitch height and evenly spaced gaps between stitches.

Note: buttonhole stitch is a variation of blanket stitch with the stitches closer together, but the tailor's buttonhole stitch is a more durable solution for mending buttonholes (see right).

TAILOR'S BUTTONHOLE STITCH

Unlike blanket and buttonhole stitch, the tailor's buttonhole stitch starts with the needle pointing in the opposite direction – away from the fabric edge – then you pull the needle and thread back up once you've made your stitch. This creates extra bumps along the edge for more stability, and there is less likelihood of the stitches unravelling if the thread breaks later on due to wear and tear. Tailors use a special thread called buttonhole twist, but it can be difficult to find; try using topstitching thread or perle cotton instead (for best results wax your thread first).

If you're mending a buttonhole with damaged threads, remove the remaining original threads before you begin. And if you're mending a buttonhole on frayed or damaged fabric, patch the area first to stabilize it.

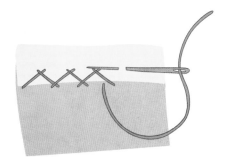

HERRINGBONE STITCH

Herringbone stitch, or catch stitch, is great for hems. For a blended mend, stitch from the inside of your garment with a single strand of matching thread and pick up only one or two fabric threads at a time. For decorative stitching, work from the right side in a contrasting colour.

WHIP STITCH

Whip stitch, or hemming stitch, is good for hems and patch edges. Whip stitches can be slanted or straight, but slanted stitches (with the needle slanted in the opposite direction) will save time because you cover more distance with each stitch.

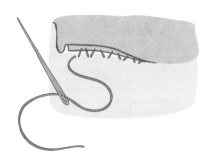

SLIP STITCH

Slip stitch is useful for mending hems and seams invisibly. Work slip stitch from the inside of your garment, making tiny stitches – picking up only a thread or two – in the main fabric and longer stitches through the folded-over hem so your stitching is less noticeable on the outside.

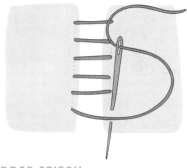

LADDER STITCH

Ladder stitch (or mattress stitch) is worked similarly to slip stitch, but stitches are the same length on each side – your thread resembles a ladder before you pull it taut. Use ladder stitch to close up seams from the outside when the inside is inaccessible (e.g. pillows or stuffed toys).

STITCH METHODS

 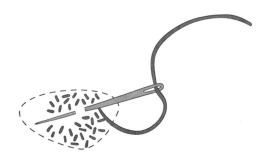

EYELETS

Eyelets are holes made into features; the stitching stabilizes the holes and prevents them from getting bigger. To make an eyelet, trim your hole with small, sharp scissors if necessary to tidy up the edges. Outline the neatened hole with running stitch to secure it, then stitch around the edge of the hole as shown.

SEED STITCH

Seed stitch is an embroidery stitch that's also useful for patching – the stitching adds reinforcement and makes the fabric layers stronger. Seed stitch is great for beginners because stitches are made randomly and there's no right or wrong way to place them – a bit like running stitch without a direct path to follow.

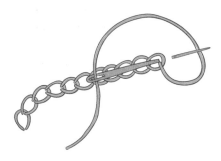

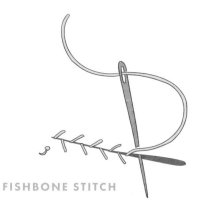

CHAIN STITCH

Although not a repair stitch, I use chain stitch often to embellish my mends. It's great for lettering, edge stitching and shape filling. With chain stitch, it's important to weave the needle down and up through your fabric in a single step (as illustrated) to secure each link of the chain; links should start and end from the same hole.

FISHBONE STITCH

Fishbone stitch is useful for stabilizing rips in fabric – usually as the first step before darning (see page 102). It can be used on its own to mend rips in leather and felt, where fraying is not an issue. Untidy tears (where the edges are frayed) will need to be patched as well.

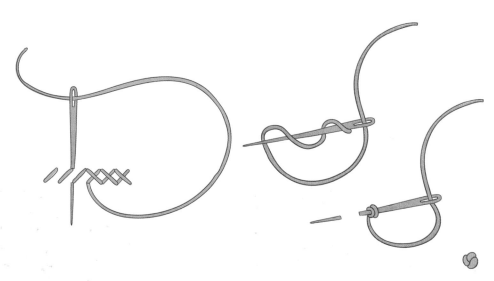

CROSS STITCH

Cross stitch is a classic embroidery stitch that is useful for mending tiny holes in T-shirts (see Erin's shirt, page 206), and for rips and seams that don't require great strength (see Leta's dress no.1, page 224) or that have been reinforced with a patch first (see Emily O's shirt, page 194). Crosses can be completed individually, or you can make a row of slanted stitches in one direction and complete the crosses in the opposite direction on your second pass. This is an easy stitch to pull too tight – an embroidery hoop can help keep woven fabric smooth and taut, and if you're stitching stretch fabric, take extra care with your stitch tension.

FRENCH KNOTS

French knots can't be used for mending on their own, but they're a great embellishment for patching and needle felting, or for revamping stains. They can be fiddly the first time you try them, but they're easy and fun with a bit of practice.

Poke your needle and thread up through your fabric and pull the thread taut. Tightly coil the thread around your needle at least twice (similar to the quilter's knot) and hold it in place with the hand not holding the needle. Hold the coiled thread near the base of the fabric while you poke the needle back down through the fabric, next to (but not in) the hole where you came up. (If you don't hold the coiled thread in place, a knot won't form and you'll have to start over.)

Vary the look by using thicker or thinner thread, more or fewer strands, or wrapping thread additional times.

Before

Mended

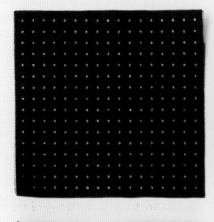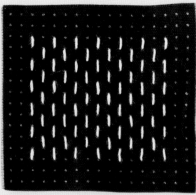

Extra fancy

A bit special

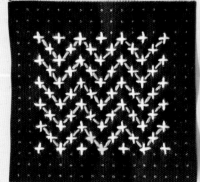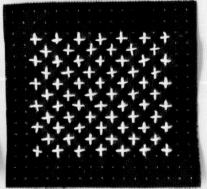

Sashiko is a Japanese embroidery technique that uses running stitch to create beautiful geometric patterns.

For sashiko-inspired mending, you'll need to add a patch first, either over or under the damaged area (over is easier for beginners). The sashiko stitches reinforce the fabric layers to make them stronger.

Sashiko stitching can be as simple as parallel lines of running stitch, or more complex patterns based on grids or circles. You can stitch traditional sashiko designs (see Anna's jeans, page 170) or make up your own stitch patterns (see Emma M's jeans, page 202).

Use a ruler and fabric-marking tool to create a grid on your fabric, or simply stitch freehand. I've tried a few fabric-marking methods and my favourites for sashiko mending are a dark Crayola washable marker (more visible than a blue water-erasable marker on denim), and specialty sashiko fabric, pre-printed with a dot grid (pictured) or stitch pattern – the printed patterns disappear when you wash them (see Resources on page 262 for suppliers, and Tools of the Trade on page 20 for more fabric-marking tools).

I love using authentic sashiko needles and threads for mending because they're well made and enjoyable to use, but they can be difficult to find outside Japan (see Resources for tips). You can get similar results with embroidery thread/floss (stranded or perle cotton) and a long embroidery needle.

For grid-based patterns, the vertical stitches are traditionally made first, followed by the horizontal, then diagonal, stitches. As with classic darning, leave little loops at the end of each stitch row to prevent shrinkage when laundering. If you're mending jeans knees or other areas that are challenging to access with a needle and thread, it can help to unpick a side seam first, then restitch it later.

There are entire books devoted to sashiko, with stitch patterns and instructions for creating them; I recommend Susan Briscoe's *The Ultimate Sashiko Sourcebook* and Jessica Marquez's *Make + Mend* if you'd like to learn more. Or search for sashiko patterns or stencils online to find one that takes your fancy.

What could go wrong?

I keep trying but I can't thread the needle.

Try switching to a different needle with a larger eye, or buy a needle threader and keep it on hand. If your eyesight or motor coordination could use a boost, you can buy easy-threading needles – they're like a needle and needle threader all in one.

I poked my finger with the needle.

It happens. If you're doing a lot of stitching or mending thick fabric, a thimble can keep your fingers safe. If you're tired, distracted or in a rush, stop stitching! Once I get going on a project, I usually don't want to stop; but after a few late-night near-misses, I made a policy to stop stitching at the first sign of sleepiness, because my hand-eye coordination declines, and so does my decision-making ability. I make sure I'm fully awake and relaxed (usually with a cup of tea) before I stitch anything now.

My stitches look wonky.

Keep practising! Sometimes I second-guess my stitching (see Should I Redo it? on page 259) but then I remember there is safety in numbers: the more stitches there are, the less noticeable the imperfections become, and they can add a lovely character to the item being mended. Before you start unpicking, wait a bit and see how your stitches look once they're part of a larger group.

My thread is a tangled mess.

Remove the threads and start again. When you cut a new length of thread, make sure it's no longer than your forearm, and try coating your thread with beeswax or thread conditioner before you thread the needle.

PRO TIPS

My needle is stuck and won't stitch through my fabric.

Try using a thimble to push the needle through, or needle-nosed pliers to pull it through.

My stitches are lumpy and not sitting flat.

Keep practising to get an even stitch tension; you want stitches to be taut but not too tight. Using an embroidery hoop or fabric stabilizer (if stitching stretch fabrics) can help with tension, too. If your stitches are too thick, try using a thinner thread or fewer strands of embroidery thread/floss.

I accidentally stitched my trouser legs/shirt sleeve shut.

Ha ha, welcome to the club! Even experienced sewists do this occasionally – usually when they're tired, distracted or in a rush. I like to put a book or piece of cardboard between fabric layers when I'm pinning or stitching to prevent this from happening.

○ A consistent stitch length and even, Goldilocks tension (not too tight, not too loose) will give you the best results. If you're having trouble making your stitches the same length, keep practising!

○ You can mend awkward things like skinny-jean legs, gloves, shoes and furniture more easily by keeping the needle action on the outside of your work. Weave the needle down and up through the fabric in one step before you pull the thread through, to avoid having to reach in and grab the needle from the inside (or taking apart your furniture).

○ For bonus enviro-points, save your thread scraps to use as stuffing for another project, such as pillows, toys, door stops and draught stoppers. ✕

TECHNIQUE:

patching

Now that you've tried hand stitching, it's time to take the next step and get patching. A patch is a new piece of fabric added to reinforce, stabilize, conceal and/or decorate existing fabric. This is a fabulous chance to use up scraps from other projects and clothing past the point of repair.

Patching is one of the easier mending techniques and can be rather quick. I like to make a few patches at once while I have my tools out and store the extras in a box for future mends. They come in handy whenever I need a quick fix or volunteer at my local Repair Cafe.

Patches are a quilting technique as well as a mending technique and there are so many ways to make them; I've included the methods I use or get asked about most often. Feel free to mix and match steps from different methods as you see fit.

THE ESSENTIALS

Clothing that needs a bit of TLC. Patching is easiest on woven, non-stretchy fabrics, but you can patch stretch fabrics with the iron-on patch, reverse appliqué or sock-patch methods.

Fabric for patching. You can make patches from just about anything: old jeans, socks, underwear (see Large Marge, page 212), pillowcases, shrunken sweaters, and even leather and lace. For best results, try to match the thickness, texture, stretch factor and fibre content of your patch with the item you're mending (e.g. linen on linen, denim or canvas on denim, wool felt on wool, silk on silk and cotton jersey on T-shirts), but feel free to mix it up with contrasting colours and prints. Ribbon is good for patching rips, and I love bias tape/binding for patching edges.

Sewing needle and thread for stitching your patch in place (see Stitching, page 41, for details).

A clothes iron for wrinkle-free fabric. If you don't have an iron it's possible to make some of the patches shown here, with a bit of finger pressing (did you know your fingers are mini clothes irons?), but I recommend borrowing a clothes iron for best results.

Something to stick your patch to the item you're mending, either temporarily or permanently:

o   **Let's stick together... forever:**
 o   For iron-on patches you'll need **fusible web**, a flat, double-sided, heat-activated glue. See Notes on Fusible Web (page 64) for details.
 o   **Fusible interfacing** is similar to fusible web but with adhesive on one side; it's best for patching on the wrong side where it won't be seen.

o   **Let's stick together... for now:**
 o   **Pins and safety pins** are so handy; I prefer safety pins for big projects because they keep my fingers safer.
 o   **Tacking/basting stitches** (for more details, see page 48). hold fabric together with thread.
 o   An ordinary **glue stick** is a clever solution that will disappear in the wash.

OPTIONAL EXTRAS

Cardstock or cereal-box cardboard for creating a patch template.

A chopstick to keep from burning your finger with the clothes iron.

Stitching aids: **a needle threader, thimble and beeswax.**

BACK

FRONT

GETTING STARTED

1. It's time for tea! Making patches is quite quick – it's stitching them in place that takes the most time – so choose your tea vessel based on how much stitching is required (a hemmed patch deserves a teapot).

2. Iron the item to be mended and your patch fabric to remove any wrinkles.

3. Get patching with one of the following methods.

Notes on Fusible Web

Fusible web is flat, double-sided, meltable glue for fabric that comes in sheets, rolls or tape. There are many brands and types available – for best results follow the instructions on your packet. My favourite is Lite Steam-a-Seam 2®: it's sticky on both sides (which makes positioning easier) and the backing papers peel away easily.

Menders seem to either love or hate it; I've outlined some thoughts here to help you decide whether to use it.

PROS:

o You can cut perfect, precise patch shapes – such as crosses, hearts, letters, circles – that would be difficult to achieve with other techniques.

o It's durable and washable.

o It saves time, which can influence whether something gets mended or not.

o It reduces fraying for raw-edge patches.

o It stops cotton jersey (T-shirt fabric) from curling and makes it easier to sew.

CONS:

o It's made of glue and is not biodegradable.

o The glue is permanent.

o The backing papers that come with it are not recyclable. Some types don't have backing papers, in which case you'll need to use your own kitchen baking paper to prevent them from sticking to your iron. One sheet of baking paper (or backing paper) can be re-used multiple times, though.

o It can make your garment stiffer (make sure to use a lightweight version if this is a concern).

o It doesn't work on woollen or fuzzy fabrics.

Feel free to use fusible web if it motivates you to get more mending done, or helps you with a desired outcome (like tricky shapes). Just use it responsibly: choose your shapes carefully and cut them as close together as possible (like Tetris) to avoid creating more waste. You can assemble leftover scraps of fusible web together (like a patchwork quilt) on the back of a fabric patch; once ironed they will all melt into the fabric and the scrap edges won't be noticeable.

1

☀ SAFETY WARNING: When ironing patches, turn off your iron's steam function and keep your fingers a safe distance away to prevent them from getting burned.

The DIY iron-on patch, AKA raw-edge appliqué, is my favourite way to patch T-shirts. I don't recommend this method for delicate fabrics, linen (which is prone to fraying) or sturdy fabrics like denim that would become too stiff.

For T-shirts (which don't fray), you could skip the fusible web if you're not a fan, but you'd need to take extra care when pinning and stitching to avoid puckering.

1. Optional: trace a design onto the backing paper of your fusible web. If you're using Steam-a-Seam® brand (shown here), which has two backing papers, trace the design on the side with a grid. Try to draw your designs as close to each other and the edge of the fusible web as possible to avoid waste.

2

4

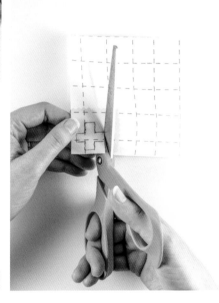

←

2. If your fusible web has two backing papers, peel back the paper without your traced design (this is important, as you'll need your design for the next step).

3. Take a scrap of fabric and stick the wrong side – the side that will be attached to your garment – to the fusible web so it covers your traced design completely.

4. Cut through the fusible web, fabric and remaining backing paper together. This part is key: cutting the fabric after it's stuck to the fusible web will give you a more precise shape and prevent fraying. For best results, use sharp scissors but not your best fabric-only scissors because the fusible web could make them dull and/or sticky.

5

6

5.   Remove the remaining backing paper (if there is one) and apply the fusible-web side of the patch to your garment like a sticker.

6.   Press the patch with your iron for a few seconds on the hottest setting your fabric can handle (use a protective cloth for synthetic or delicate fabrics if you're not sure). Do not iron directly onto fusible web or it will create a sticky mess on your iron that is difficult to remove. If you're patching a large hole, place backing paper (or kitchen baking paper) under the hole to protect your ironing board, or inside your garment if you're mending trousers or a sleeve (as shown) to avoid sealing them shut.

After

←

7. Stitch through both layers of fabric around 2–3mm (⅛in) in from the edge of the patch. For T-shirts, I like backstitch because it has a bit of stretch to it. Some types of fusible web claim you don't need to sew them, but if you're mending something that's stretchy or going to be worn and washed frequently, stitching prevents the patch from peeling away at the edges.

SAFETY WARNING: Don't forget to turn off the steam function when ironing patch edges. You can use a chopstick to keep your fingers a safe distance away.

Turned-edge appliqué is stitched onto the right side of your fabric, with edges turned under to prevent fraying. This method is good for delicate fabrics and clothes that are likely to get lots of wear and tear.

In the quilting technique known as English paper piecing (EPP), geometric shapes are created using paper templates, and the edges formed with stitches.

The shapes are hand-stitched together to make a larger quilt. This is my punk version of EPP, using an iron and a cardboard or cardstock template (you can find printable hexagon templates online). Cardboard is more durable than paper and can be ironed and re-used many times. Here I've shown how I make a hexagon, but for an easier patch, make a rectangle instead – with or without a template – and follow the remaining steps for attaching it and sewing it in place.

If you need a patch that looks good from both sides, try the hemmed patch instead.

→

←

1. Cut your preferred shape from your patch fabric, leaving an extra 1cm (⅜in) border around the edges (known as a seam allowance) for turning under later. For hexagons, cut a slightly larger hexagon shape (best for thick fabrics to avoid bulk), or be lazy like me and just cut a square (pictured). Proper quilters use a much smaller seam allowance but they're not following my punk EPP method – the extra seam allowance makes this method quicker, easier and safer for your fingers.

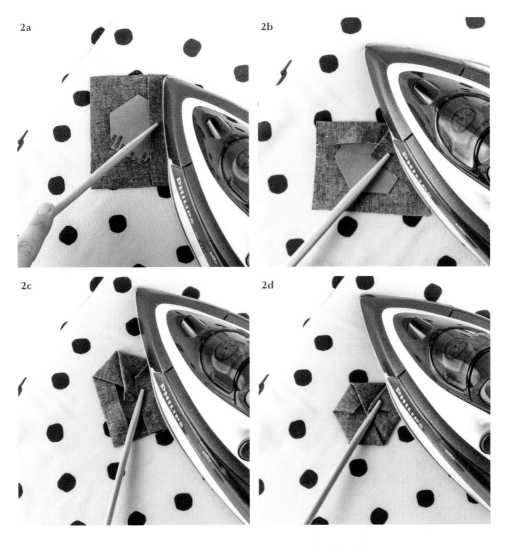

2a

2b

2c

2d

2. Using your template as a guide, iron the edges of your patch one at a time as shown, using a chopstick to hold the patch in place and keep your fingers out of danger. You can finger-press each crease before you get to the ironing board to make it easier.

(If you're not using a template, turn the edges with an iron by the same amount on each side.) Once you've turned all the edges, flip the patch and give it a good press on the other side.

→

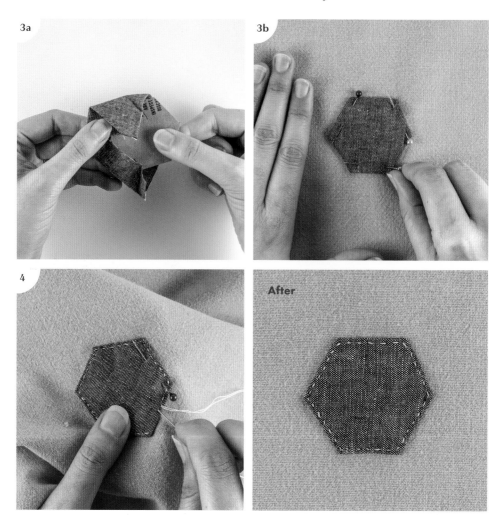

3a

3b

4

After

3. Remove the template, then pin, glue or tack/baste your patch in place.

4. Stitch through both layers of fabric. For edge stitches, try whip stitch, running stitch, blanket stitch, backstitch or chain stitch. Or use seed stitch or lines of running stitch throughout the patch.

5. Remove any pins or tacking/basting stitches.

2

The method shown here works best on T-shirts, felted wool blankets and other items that won't fray when you cut them. If you are mending something that frays (which is most things), turn under the edges of the hole and stitch them in place with whip stitch, or skip ahead to the deluxe version, the hemmed patch, where all edges are turned under. You can also use fusible web for this technique, cutting a window in your fusible web before you apply it (if you don't cut a window you'll have a gluey mess in the middle).

1. Cut a fabric patch much larger than the damaged area (you'll trim the excess later).

2. Using your preferred fabric-marking tool, draw your outer stitch line and inner cut line with a 2–3mm (⅛in) gap in between. (I used two different coins here to make it easier.) This step is optional but it prevents you from removing too much fabric accidentally, making the final steps less scary.

→

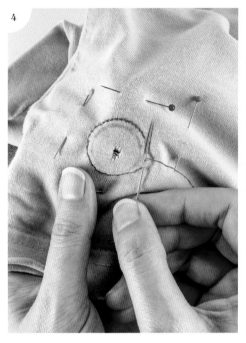

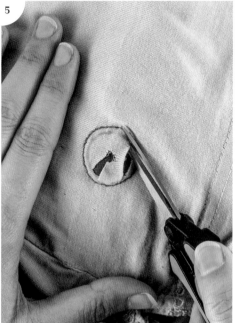

←

3. Centre your patch fabric underneath the area to be mended and pin, tack/baste or glue it in place around the edges. (If you're using a glue stick or fusible web, be careful to glue the edges only, not the centre where you'll be removing fabric later, to avoid a gluey mess.)

4. Stitch through both layers of fabric, by hand or machine, along the outer stitch line. For T-shirts I like backstitch because it's strong and can stretch.

5. Carefully trim the damaged area along the inner cut line to make a window.

6

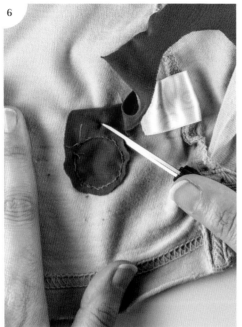

After

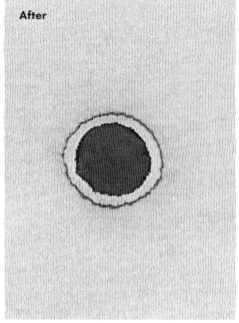

6. Turn the garment inside-out and
    trim the excess patch fabric, leaving
    a 2–3mm (⅛in) or more border
    around your stitch line. Turn the
    garment right side out, remove any
    fabric markings and give the patch
    a good press with a steam iron for a
    few seconds to smooth it out.

2

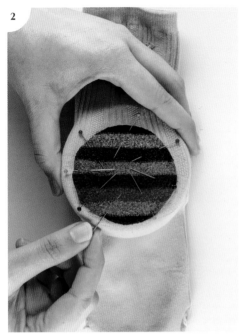

3

Darning is the best method for mending socks, but darning thin, machine-knit socks can be time-consuming and eye-straining. Thank goodness there's a better (lazier) way — you can patch them instead!

This method is similar to reverse appliqué (page 73) but the removal of damaged fabric is optional here.

Note: you'll need a similarly soft and stretchy jersey fabric for patches, ideally from another sock. You can designate a pair of socks in bad shape (or a single sock that's lost its mate) as your 'donor' patch source.

1. Optional: trim the damaged area, leaving a tidy hole.

2. Turn the sock to be mended inside-out. Cut a round patch from similar fabric (see intro note, left) that's larger than the damaged area, adding at least a 1cm (⅜in) border. (I used a jar lid to trace matching circle patches.) Align the patch and sock along the grainline, matching any ribbing, and pin in place. If your patch is in a relatively flat part of the sock, insert a jar lid for easier, tidier stitching, and to prevent from accidentally stitching your sock shut. If it's in a curved

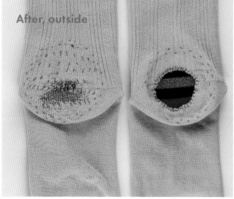

After, outside

After, inside

spot, use a darning mushroom or other round object to help you hold the shape while you pin and stitch.

3. Stitch the patch along the edge with herringbone stitch (page 51), using thin yarn or mending wool if you're mending thin woolly socks, or 1-2 strands of embroidery thread/floss or sewing thread if you're sewing cotton socks. Remove the pins as you stitch. To avoid knots under your feet, start and finish each length of thread/yarn by taking

a few backstitches in the same spot, then weave in the ends through the fabric or other stitches.

4. Turn the sock right side out and continue stitching the sock and patch together to reinforce them. Whip stitch (shown here on both socks) is somewhat stretchy and good for hole edges and reinforcing threadbare areas; herringbone and backstitch also stretch and can be used for hole edges. (Avoid running stitch, which has no stretch.)

METHOD: HEMMED PATCH

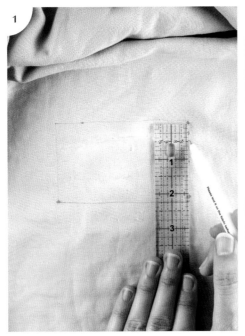

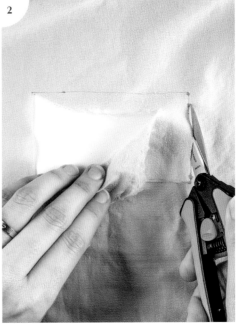

This is a traditional patch method for woven fabrics that get washed often; it's strong and looks great from both sides. The first time I attempted a hemmed patch, I got pretty frustrated and never wanted to make one again, but after attending a mending workshop by Tom Van Deijnen (page 252), I picked up a few helpful tips and now I adore them. Classic mending books show you how to make a hemmed patch in two or three illustrations, but they assume you have a bit of sewing knowledge and experience already. I've broken down the process into more steps here to make it easier, so you can fall in love with hemmed patches more quickly than I did.

1. Optional: mark a rectangle or square shape around the damaged area with a fabric-marking tool. This will be your cut line.

2. With a pair of scissors, carefully remove the damaged fabric to make a window.

3. Clip each corner the same length at a 45-degree angle (I made 7mm/¼in cuts here).

4. Remove any fabric markings. Turn under each edge (my seam allowance was 5mm/¼in here) and press with an iron.

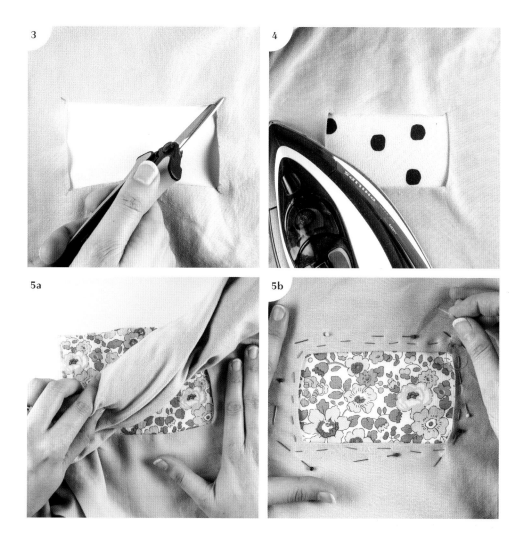

5.   Centre your patch fabric (right side up) under the window you've just made and pin and/or tack/baste around the edges to hold it in place. For sturdy fabrics, pins are enough, but this sheet is extra-soft and wriggly so I chose to add tacking/ basting stitches for neater edges. (I used Liberty Tana Lawn fabric because it's soft and thin just like the sheet, and it's expensive, so using up my scraps for patches makes me feel extra-fancy.)

→

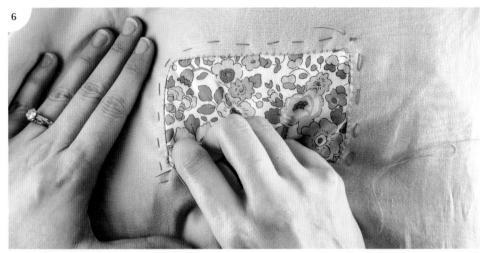

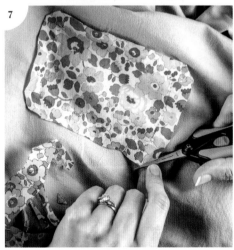

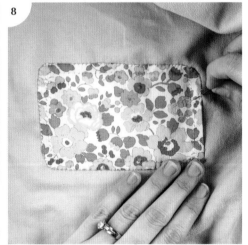

←

6. Whip stitch around the edge of the patch window, making extra stitches at each corner to prevent fraying.

7. Remove any pins and tacking/basting stitches and flip your item to the wrong side. Trim the excess patch fabric (I left a 1cm/⅜in border) and clip the corners.

8. Turn under the edges and whip stitch them in place. Press the finished patch with an iron for a few seconds to smooth it out.

FRONT

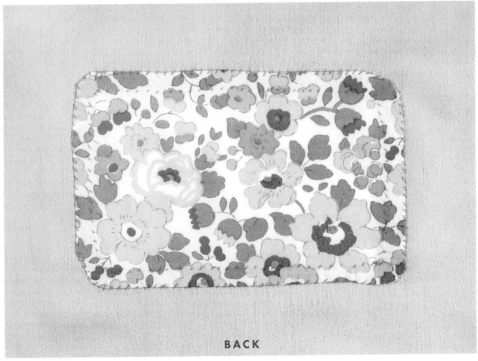

BACK

METHOD: SECRET PATCH

2

3

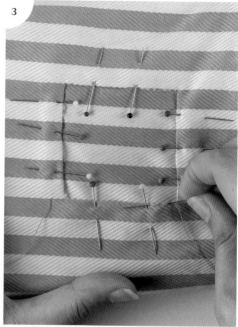

A secret patch, also known as an oversewn or inset patch, is a handy invisible-mending trick to have up your sleeve (ha!). The optical illusion works best on thin and lightweight woven fabric with a printed pattern. The keys to invisibility are good pattern matching (it's best to use the same fabric) and tiny, even stitches. Shirt cuffs, shoulder linings and large seam allowances are good patch sources; or shorten sleeves or hemlines and use the leftovers. Invisibility often comes at the expense of strength; if your garment needs to be washed and worn often, opt for a hemmed patch (page 78) or turned-edge appliqué (page 69) instead.

1. Prep your garment using steps 1-4 of the hemmed-patch method.

2. Cut a patch from a hidden part of the garment, matching the fabric print and grainline and adding a minimum 1cm (⅜in) border (when matching patterns, the more fabric, the better). Use the hole as your guide or make a cardboard template (see Fussy cutting, page 85).

3. Match your patch fabric right-side up under the hole and pin it in place, then slip-tack/baste (temporary slip stitch, page 51) along the edges. (I inserted a book in the sleeve here to avoid pinning or stitching it shut.) Remove the pins when you're finished.

4. Turn the garment to the wrong side and fold back each fabric join, one at a time, with right sides together as shown. Using one strand of matching sewing thread, overstitch the join (like whip stitch, page 51, on the edge) with tiny, even stitches — picking up only a thread or two of each piece of fabric at a time.

Take two or three stitches at each corner to prevent fraying, continue overstitching each side of the patch, then remove the tacking/basting thread.

5. Trim the excess patch fabric, leaving a 1cm (⅜in) border, and clip the corners. Press with a steam iron.

6. Optional: finish the raw edges of the fabric with pinking shears, or overstitch them if the fabric is likely to fray (see next page).

7. Patch over the site where you removed the secret-patch fabric.

METHOD: SECRET PATCH

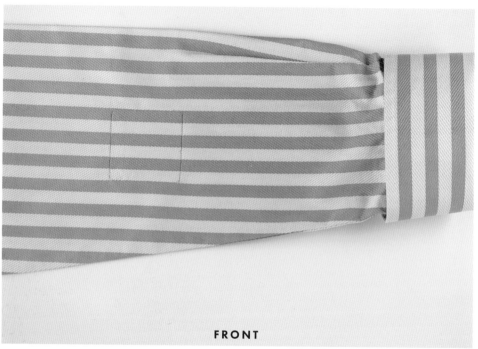

FRONT

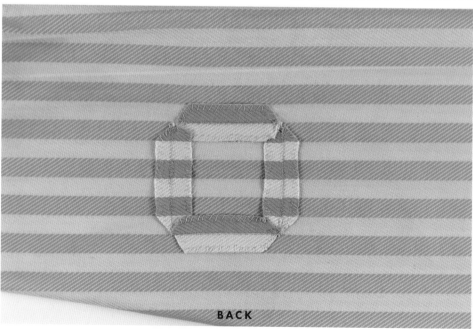

BACK

Fun with Fussy Cutting

Fussy cutting is a classic patch-making technique used by quilters to intentionally feature – or avoid – a specific section of fabric. It's perfect for bold prints and for cherry-picking the best bits from preloved fabric with small stains, with holes or some other damage.

To create a fussy-cutting template, draw your desired patch shape and size onto cardstock or cardboard, then draw a 1cm (⅜in) border around it. Cut along both lines to create a frame. The window in the centre is the finished patch size; the frame is your seam allowance – the excess

fabric that will get folded underneath. (If you're following the turned-edge appliqué method on page 69, you can save the cut-out inner piece to use as your ironing template.)

To use: centre the template on fabric over your preferred design element and align it with the item's grainline and/or any strong printed lines (such as stripes or checks). Use a fabric-marking tool to trace the template along the outer border, then cut fabric along the traced line for use in one of the patch methods on pages 64–84.

What could go wrong?

My patch is an odd shape.

Try cutting a template from cardstock or cardboard first, or trace your shape onto the patch fabric with a fabric-marking tool before you cut it.

My patch is lumpy.

Pin or tack/baste your patch in place before stitching it (or pin then tack/baste) to make it nice and flat. Pinning might seem like a chore but it always pays off in the end. Even tension is necessary for good stitching. To prevent from pulling your stitches too tight on woven fabrics, try using an embroidery hoop.

My patch is, *ahem*, too visible.

Try the secret patch method or try patching from the wrong side of your garment instead, using fusible web and same-colour fabric. Black dress trousers with a small hole can be mended nearly invisibly this way.

I poked my finger with the needle.

It happens. If you're stitching through thick layers of fabric, a thimble or needle-nosed pliers can help you move the needle more easily and keep your fingers safe. If you're tired, distracted or in a rush, stop sewing! Once I get going on a project I usually don't want to stop, but after a few late-night near misses I made a policy to stop sewing at the first sign of sleepiness, because my hand-eye coordination declines, and so does my decision-making ability. I make sure I'm fully awake and relaxed (usually with a cup of tea) before I stitch anything now.

I poked my finger with pins.

It took me a few decades to realize safety pins are called safety pins for a reason! They're a mender's best friend.

EXPERIMEND

I burnt my finger with the iron.

Ouch! Run your finger under cold water immediately. Next time turn off the steam function and use a chopstick to keep your fingers a safe distance away.

My iron is covered in sticky goo.

Don't iron directly onto fusible web or it will create a sticky mess that is difficult to remove. Try ironing a piece of kitchen paper to remove the glue. In future, cut your patch fabric and fusible web at the same time to ensure there's no exposed fusible web to worry about.

My needle is stuck and won't stitch through my fabric.

Try using a thimble to push the needle through, or needle-nosed pliers to pull it through.

o Leather and lace can make fun patches. Leather is a good extra-strength solution (e.g. elbow patches, and Leta's dress no.2, page 228), and lace patches are great for covering stains and holes on thin knitwear that would be challenging to darn. Use lace that has a motif you can cut out with scissors (not doily-style lace, which will unravel), and for bonus enviro-points use leather offcuts.

o Make your own embroidered iron-on patch with embroidery and fusible web. Embroider one or two layers of fabric, add another layer of fabric on the back with fusible web, then trim around the edges and stitch your new patch in place. ✕

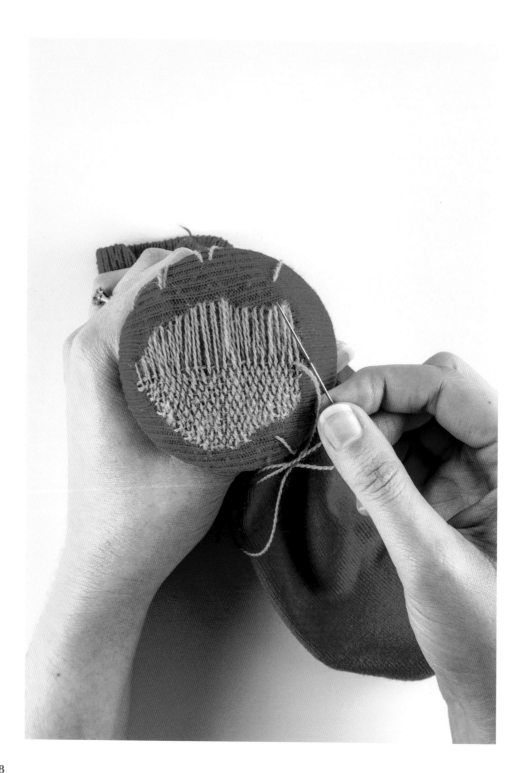

TECHNIQUE:

darning

Darning is weaving new fabric on a very small scale, using yarn or thread. Some people find it challenging the first time – you're making new fabric (!) and your brain might say, 'Excuse me, but how is that possible?' – but keep going because it's one of the most useful techniques you can learn.

Don't give up if your first attempt doesn't look how you'd hoped. Just like the first pancake, your first darn will probably be a bit wonky, but you will learn so much and your second darn will be much neater. All it takes is a little practice.

Just like stitching, darning is slow, repetitive work and requires concentration, but it's great for getting into the flow and achieving a more relaxed state of mind. And like stitching, it requires only a small toolkit, so it's a great way to mend on the go (my student Kat has been teaching strangers to darn while riding the bus!).

Fun fact: no knots are needed for darning. All loose yarn ends ('tails') are woven in at the end, ensuring darned items such as socks and gloves are smooth and not irritating to wear.

WHAT YOU NEED

THE ESSENTIALS

Clothing that needs TLC. Classic darning, surface darning, Scotch darning and honeycomb darning work well on woven and knit fabrics; Swiss darning is suitable for knitted items only.

Yarn for darning. For best results match the thickness, texture and fibre composition with the item you're mending. For blended mends, a good colour match is key.

o   Mending wool is usually a mixture of wool and nylon for added strength; it comes in small lengths.

o   Knitting yarn is easy to find and great for hand-knitted items. Some yarns can be separated into thinner strands (plies) successfully, but others need all of their plies to hold together.

o   Sock yarn is made especially for knitting socks and is often a mixture of wool and nylon for added strength. Variegated sock yarn is fun because the colours change while you work.

o   Crewel wool is perfect for darning but can be harder to find (see Resources, page 262, for tips).

o   Tapestry wool is thicker and good for mending chunky hand-knits.

o   Stranded cotton embroidery thread/floss has 6 strands and a slight sheen. You choose how many strands to use at a time, depending on what you're darning. It splits easily, making darning more challenging; use beeswax to bind strands together.

o   Tapestry cotton is matt and not meant to be separated. It can be useful for darning thick cotton items such as socks when a sheen is not desired.

o   Small bits of yarn sometimes come with new clothes. They are perfect for darning – that's why they exist!

Needles to suit your yarn and fabric. Long embroidery needles are good for woven fabric and blunt tapestry needles are good for hand-knitted items. Ideally your needle should be longer than the damaged area so you can load an entire row of stitches on it at one time.

OPTIONAL EXTRAS

Scissors for snipping yarn. (You can break knitting wool by hand instead; the fuzzy ends will blend in better.)

Stability aids such as darning mushrooms, oranges and embroidery hoops can help hold the shape of the item you're mending. Paper (tacked/basted in place) is a good option for delicate items and extensive rescues.

Beeswax or thread conditioner for waxing cotton thread prone to splitting.

A needle threader makes threading your needle easier; try a specialty embroidery or tapestry threader for thick yarns.

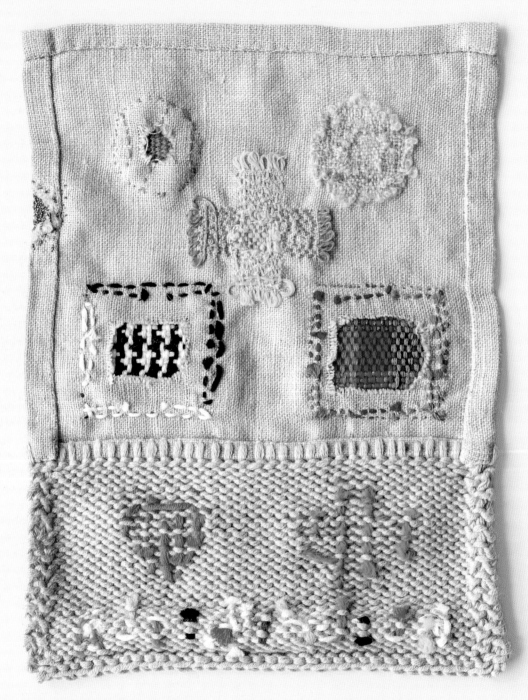

BACK

92

FRONT

GETTING STARTED

2

1. Make a pot of tea. Darning is a slow, meditative activity; it's nice to stay in the flow and not have to get up midway to refill your teacup.

2. Optional: if you're darning a hole, snip off any loose threads and trim the hole into a tidier shape before you begin. If you're darning a threadbare area that's not yet a hole (socks often wear down to a thin nylon skeleton), keep those threads intact; they'll provide a framework for your darn and make a faster and easier job of it.

3. For classic darning, turn your garment inside-out. For all other methods, work right side out.

4. Optional: secure the item to be mended over a darning mushroom (with an elastic band if desired), orange, embroidery hoop or piece of paper. The fabric should lie flat (or curved if it's a sock or glove) naturally and not be stretched out.

5. Thread your needle with a single strand of yarn, roughly the length of your forearm; don't make a knot. Optional: wax cotton thread to make it easier to work with.

METHOD: CLASSIC DARNING

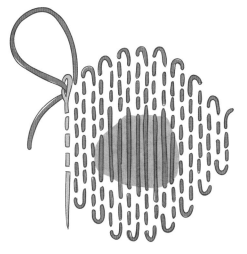

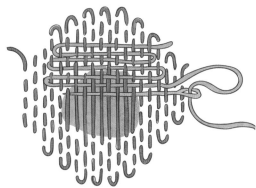

This is my desert-island darn; if you only learn one method, make it this one. It's strong and versatile – you can use it on knitwear and woven fabric.

A key feature of the classic darn (AKA stocking darn) is tiny loops at the end of each row, which offset any shrinkage that might occur in the wash. This method is traditionally worked from the wrong side of a garment (in matching thread/yarn for maximum invisibility), so when you wear the mended item the loops are not visible.

It's okay if your darning is a bit untidy; as long as you do your best work directly over the hole (because that's what will be visible from the right side) – especially if you're darning socks – it will prevent toes from poking through.

Classic darns on knit fabric won't be as stretchy as the item you're mending. If stretch is important, weave your second pass of darning stitches on the bias (see Fabric 101, page 26) or choose a Swiss darn, stocking-web darn or Scotch darn instead.

METHOD: CLASSIC DARNING

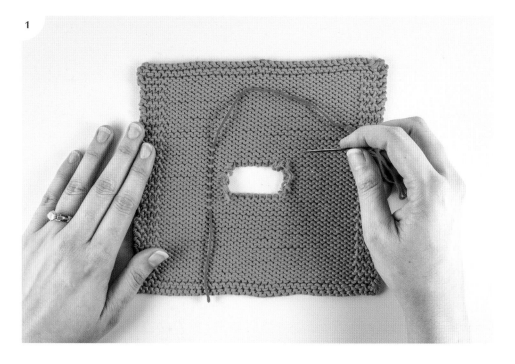

FIRST PASS

1. Leaving a margin of at least 1cm (⅜in) around your hole and a yarn tail at the end, start in one corner and make a vertical row of running stitches. Follow the shape of your hole as best as you can, and align your stitches with the grainline of the fabric you're mending (see Fabric 101, page 26); for knitted items, you can weave through the back of every other purl loop (pictured); for woven and/or threadbare items, you can use the existing threads to guide you.

2. Now head in the opposite direction and make a row of stitches next to the first row. Ideally, your rows should be touching with no gaps, unless you're darning something with a loose weave. (The diagram on page 95 has spaced the rows so they're easier to see, but pack your rows together as closely as you can.) Pull the needle and yarn through most of the way, leaving a little loop at the end. The stitches should be taut and only the loop should have slack. I like to hold down the loop end with my finger while pulling the needle and yarn through with my opposite hand, which gives me more control.

3

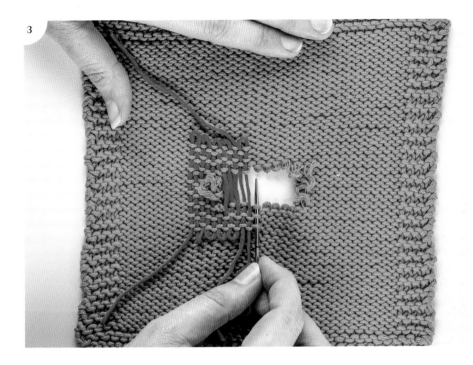

3. Continue stitching rows close together until you reach the opposite corner or edge from where you started. Whenever you run out of yarn, leave a tail at the end, which you can weave in later. Then continue where you left off with another length of yarn.

→

METHOD: CLASSIC DARNING

4

←

SECOND PASS

4. Switch yarn colours, if desired – I've changed from red to white. Turn your work by 180 degrees and begin weaving over and under the stitches you made previously. You don't need to start at the edge for the second pass; you can start and end a few rows either side of your hole.

5

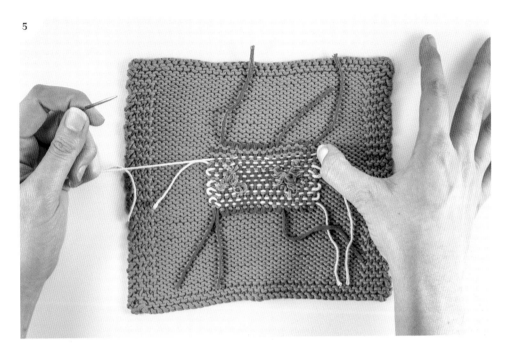

5. Continue stitching and weaving, staggering your stitches over and under every row until you reach the opposite corner or edge of your design.

→

METHOD: CLASSIC DARNING

←

6. Finish by weaving in any yarn tails. You can use them to make new rows or reinforce the surrounding fabric. Snip or tear off the excess yarn once the tail has been woven through a few stitches. Press your mended fabric with a steam iron, if desired, for a smoother finish.

FRONT

BACK

METHOD: CLASSIC DARNING ON AN L-SHAPED TEAR

2

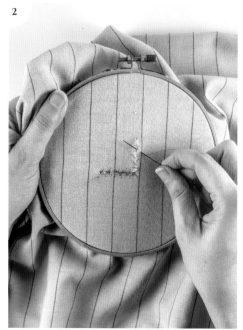

3

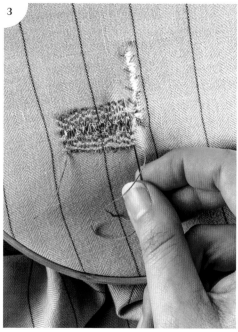

This method works best for clean tears; for ragged tears, add scrap fabric from behind for reinforcement then darn, or try a hemmed patch (page 78) instead.

1. Secure the fabric to be mended with an embroidery hoop (taking care not to overstretch the fabric), or tack/baste it to a piece of paper to keep it taut and flat.

2. Stitch the tear closed with fishbone stitch (see page 52), taking care to start and end your stitches in strong, undamaged parts of the fabric to prevent further damage.

FIRST PASS

3. Darn across one rip towards the corner, extending well beyond each end of the rip.

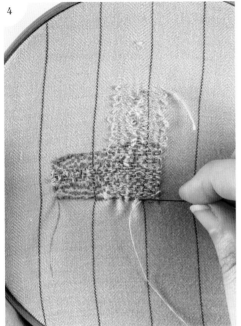

4

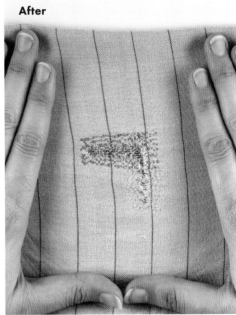

After

SECOND PASS

4. Darn across the other rip towards the corner, weaving over and under the first pass of stitches when you get there. (Here I extended my second pass of darning along the first rip for extra coverage, but if you have a clean tear this won't be necessary.)

5. Weave all yarn tails into the surrounding fabric and press with a steam iron if desired.

METHOD: SURFACE DARNING

1

Surface darning, also known as needle weaving, is similar to classic darning but your weaving floats on the surface and is not fully integrated into the surrounding fabric. This makes it slightly more challenging (it's harder to keep your rows close together and your weaving even without that integration), not as strong, and unattractive from the wrong side where the damage is still visible. On the plus side, it's worked from the right side of a garment and all of your stitches are visible, so you can easily see what the finished mend will look like, and you can make more complex, interesting shapes and weave patterns.

1. If you're mending a large hole, secure the border with running stitch.

2

3

FIRST PASS

2. With about a 1cm (⅜in) margin all around and starting in one corner, begin weaving rows across the hole or threadbare area in a compact zigzag pattern, taking a small stitch at each edge to anchor before crossing over in the opposite direction. Continue until the hole or area is completely covered. If you're darning a long shape, work the shorter rows first for more stability. Whenever you run out of yarn, leave a tail at the end; don't make a knot. Then continue where you left off with another length of yarn.

SECOND PASS

3. Switch colours, if desired. Turn your work 90 degrees and begin weaving over and under the rows you made previously, and continue taking a small stitch at the end of every row. To avoid splitting yarn, you can pass your needle through by its eye instead of the point. After each row you can use the needle to help push your rows closer together, which will give you a better finished result.

→

METHOD: SURFACE DARNING

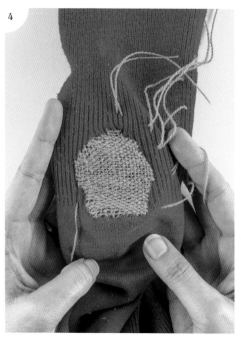

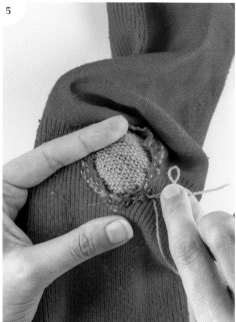

4. Continue stitching and weaving until you reach the opposite corner or edge of your design.

5. Turn the garment inside-out and weave all the tails into the surrounding fabric. If you leave long tails you can use them to reinforce the surrounding area and make it stronger.

METHOD: SWISS DARNING

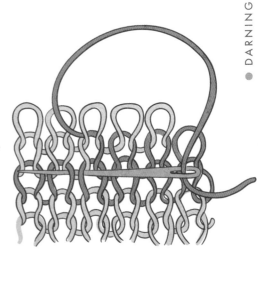
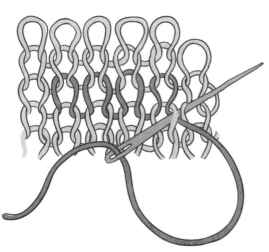

Swiss darning is a reinforcement technique for threadbare knitwear *before* full-blown holes appear. It's known as duplicate stitch in the knitting world because you follow the original knit stitches (which look like Vs), using them as your guide to create new patterns or blocks of colour. (I've made a heart shape in the steps on the following pages to show you what's possible.)

Swiss darning can be invisible if you use the same yarn or a good match. It's great for reinforcing socks and other knits, but more challenging and time-consuming for fixing holes (see stocking-web darning, page 111).

For best results, start and end your Swiss darning on undamaged stitches – at least one good row above and below, and at least one or two good stitches on each side of the damaged area.

Swiss darning can be eye-straining if you're mending fine, machine-knit clothing; if I can't see the individual knit stitches without squinting, I'll choose classic darning, surface darning or Scotch darning instead, which are easier on the eyes and require less precision.

→

METHOD: SWISS DARNING

1. Anchor your yarn: insert your needle into the fabric from the right side, somewhere below where you'd like to begin. Come up through the bottom of your first stitch (V) and leave a tail at the bottom, which you'll weave in later.

2. Make a stitch: poke your needle into the fabric one row above your starting point, carefully following the full V height to make a whole stitch, not a half stitch. Stitch across, behind the middle of the V above. Complete the stitch by poking down at the bottom of the V where you started (pictured). Then bring your needle and yarn back up at the bottom of your next V stitch.

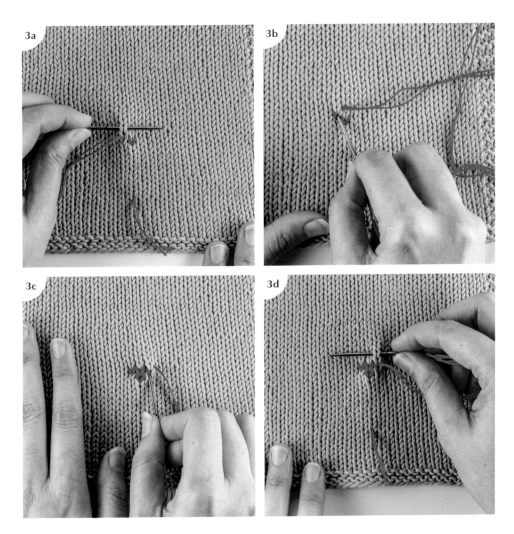

3a

3b

3c

3d

3. Make a row. Here we're making a heart so our first row has only one stitch, but if you're making a rectangle or other shape, keep making stitches until your first row is complete. Then move up one row and make the next row of stitches in the opposite direction.

→

METHOD: SWISS DARNING

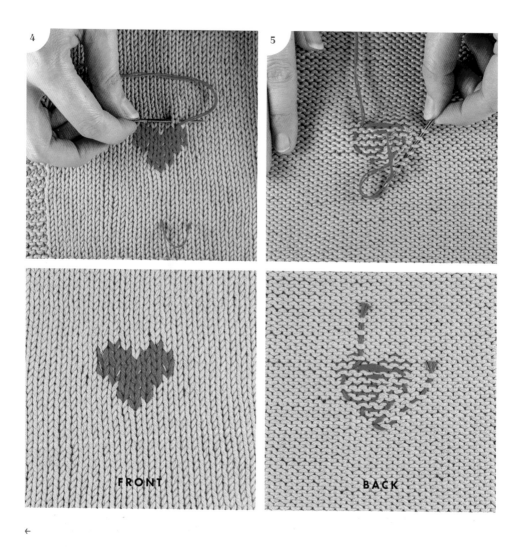

4.   Keep adding new rows of stitches until your pattern is complete.

5.   Turn the garment inside-out and weave all the tails behind the darn or in the surrounding fabric, weaving through every other purl loop. Press with a steam iron if desired.

VARIATION: STOCKING-WEB DARNING

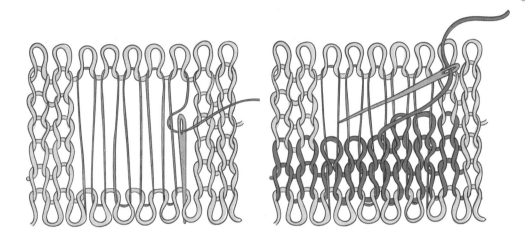

Swiss darning needs an existing knit structure to follow; if you're mending a hole, you'll need to create a temporary structure from sewing thread first. Note: this method is not recommended for beginners; if you're mending a hole and are new to darning, try classic darning instead.

1. Secure (but don't cut) any loose yarn ends to the back and fix any dropped stitches (see page 162) so you have a rectangular hole with level rows of loops across the top and bottom. You can use safety pins to secure the loops and prevent them from unravelling further.

2. Create a staggered web of thread, connecting the top and bottom loops as shown – similar to ladder stitch (see page 51). Keep the thread taut but not too tight so the fabric lies flat.

3. Swiss darn with yarn over the hole's bottom row, starting and ending at least one stitch beyond the hole. Make the next row in the opposite direction, using the web to guide you as shown and replicating the original knit tension. For the last row, graft the new and old sections together with yarn, the same way you made the web. Remove the thread and weave in any yarn tails.

111

METHOD: SCOTCH DARNING

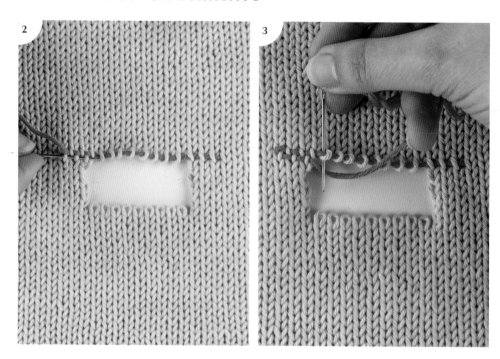

Blanket stitch (page 50) can be used to fill holes and reinforce threadbare areas on knits and woven fabrics. Blanket-stitch darns are sturdy, stretchy and forgiving; it's easy to add or skip a stitch spontaneously if you need to.

Blanket-stitch darning has many variations and names: it's often called Scotch darning when rows are stacked like a brick wall, and honeycomb darning when reinforcing threadbare fabric in a spiral pattern. In needle lace it's known as corded single Brussels stitch or corded buttonhole stitch. If you're interested in creating your own lace to fill holes, it's worth exploring needle-lace techniques.

FIRST ROW (ORANGE)

1. Working right to left, secure the top of the hole or just above it with a row of running stitch – extending beyond each side of the hole by 2-3 stitches – and leave a yarn tail, which you'll weave in later. This step creates a 'support bar' of yarn for your first blanket stitches to hold on to.

2. Staying in the same row, turn and stitch left to right – stitching between each edge stitch you made in step 1 – until you reach the hole. (It looks like another row here but

it's not; I've picked up the other leg of each knit stitch (V).) Avoid pulling too tightly as you turn.

3. Make a series of evenly spaced blanket stitches across the hole. With each blanket stitch your needle should catch two bits of yarn: the knit-stitch loop above or some of the fabric, and the support bar. (One blanket stitch per knit stitch is a good starting point; for denser darning try two blanket stitches per knit stitch.) Finish the row by stitching between the edge stitches you made in step 1.

MIDDLE ROWS (BLUE)

4. Turn and thread a support bar of yarn across the row below, taking a few running stitches at each edge. Whenever you run out of yarn or want to change colours, leave a tail at the end of the row; don't make a knot. Then continue where you left off with a new length of yarn.

5. Turn and stitch through the same row like you did in steps 2 and 3, but with each new blanket stitch catching the bottom of the blanket stitch above it and the support bar.

→

METHOD: SCOTCH DARNING

←

6. Repeat steps 4 and 5, moving back and forth like a typewriter – threading support bars from right to left and blanket stitching from left to right – until you get to the last row.

LAST ROW (ORANGE)

7. In the last row, each blanket stitch should catch three bits of yarn: the blanket stitch above it, the support bar and a knit-stitch loop or bit of fabric from the bottom edge.

8. When you're finished, turn the garment inside-out and weave the tails through the back of the stitches you've just created or the surrounding fabric. Press with a steam iron if desired.

AFTER, FRONT

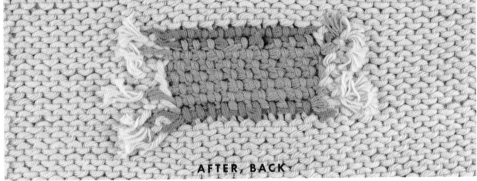

AFTER, BACK

VARIATION SUGGESTIONS:

o Add rows of running stitch to the top and bottom of your darn for extra reinforcement.

o Experimend with stitch width, row height, row width or stitch patterns (adding or skipping stitches each row for decorative lace-like effect).

o Set up all of your support bars at the same time – before you begin any blanket stitching. Then blanket-stitch your way across the bars, working alternating rows from left to right and right to left (yes, you can blanket-stitch in reverse!).

o If darning a threadbare area, skip the support bars (or add only as needed), catching the blanket stitch above and some of the threadbare fabric with each blanket stitch (see next page).

o Vary the spacing of your edge stitches or hide them inside your garment.

o Darn in a spiral pattern (see Honeycomb Darning, next page).

VARIATION: HONEYCOMB DARNING (THREADBARE)

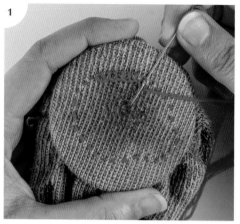

1

2

After

1. Outline the area to be mended with running stitch or backstitch see (page 48), then make a ring of evenly spaced blanket stitches (see page 50), using the outline as your border. Complete the ring by stitching down through the first blanket stitch you made.

2. Start a new ring of blanket stitches inside the first ring, with each stitch catching the blanket stitch above it. Repeat as necessary. (As the rings get smaller you'll need fewer stitches; skip stitches as required.)

3. Turn the garment inside-out and weave the tails through the back of the stitches you've just created or the surrounding fabric.

VARIATION: HONEYCOMB DARNING (HOLE)

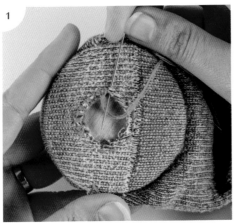

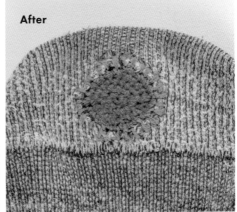

1. Secure the hole with running stitch or backstitch. Then make a ring of evenly spaced blanket stitches using the outline as your border.

2. Finish the ring by poking through the first blanket stitch, then create a support frame in four or more sections by anchoring the yarn every so often through a blanket stitch as shown.

3. Make a new ring of blanket stitches inside the first ring, with each stitch catching the support frame and blanket stitch above it.

4. Repeat steps 2 and 3 until the hole is filled, skipping stitches and supports as you go if not required.

5. Turn the garment inside-out and weave the tails through the back of the stitches or surrounding fabric.

EXPERIMEND

- Darning is great for using up odd scraps of yarn; my student Kyllie used six teabag strings to darn a hole in a tea towel!

- The over-one, under-one weave pattern shown throughout this section is known as basketweave, but you can experimend with different weave patterns and colour combinations (surface darning is the best way to show off fancy weave patterns). For pattern inspiration, check out *Needle Weaving Techniques for Hand Embroidery* by Hazel Blomkamp.

- You don't need to strictly follow all the steps in each darning method – you can mix up elements of classic darning and surface darning together to get your desired result.

PRO TIPS

- If you're new to darning and want to mend something invisibly, practise first on scrap fabric with yarn in a contrasting colour (or colours). It will be much easier to see what you're doing and where you need to stitch next. Then, once you get the hang of it, you can try invisible mending.

- If you're playing the game of 'yarn chicken' while darning – stubbornly refusing to start a new length of yarn and taking a chance that the current piece will see you through to the end – don't do it in the middle of a row. Start and end new lengths of yarn at the edges of your darn and weave in the tails later.

- Perfectly straight edges can make the surrounding fabric more susceptible to further damage. Try a round darn or a wavy shape instead to distribute any potential strain.

- You can use a glass jar instead of a darning mushroom for darning sleeves (thanks to my student Geraldine for this tip).

What could go wrong?

My darn is lumpy.

Check your garment up close and the yarn that you used: are they the same thickness? A common mistake is using yarn that's too thick, which can make your mending stiff and lumpy. Try separating your yarn and darning with only one ply (if the yarn is strong enough and can be separated) or switching to thinner yarn.

My darn is too tight or too loose.

For best results, keep your fabric taut and stable but not too tight, or you risk the fabric ripping again. An embroidery hoop can help but if you're mending a large hole or rip it's easy to overstretch the fabric, which turns your darning into a floppy mess once the hoop is removed. For some projects a piece of paper is a better stabilizer because there's less risk of overstretching. Also, the loops I recommend in the classic darning section might seem unnecessary, but think of them as your little helpers: they offset any shrinkage that might occur in the wash, and you can pull on them gently to adjust your darn and make it tighter or looser if necessary.

I can see through my darn.

For best results, pack your rows together as closely as possible, with no gaps in between. You can go back and add a few more rows after you've finished, keeping in mind that a woven pattern will be out of sync. (That said, if you're darning dark fabric no one will notice, so go for it!)

I can't see where I'm weaving.

Real talk: sometimes you can't see what you're doing when you're darning because the surrounding fabric is fuzzy, highly textured and/or dark. Just do your best.

My yarn is splitting and I keep weaving through it.

If your yarn has multiple strands or plies, it's easy to unintentionally weave *through* it rather than over or under it. Embroidery thread/floss tends to split when overworked; coating it with beeswax can help. Or try separating your yarn and darning with only one ply (if the yarn is strong enough and can be separated) or switching to another yarn entirely. For surface darning, try weaving with the eye of the needle rather than the point. ✕

TECHNIQUE:

needle felting

Needle felting, also known as dry felting, transforms wool fibres into felt using a special notched needle and friction. Needle felting is more commonly used to make three-dimensional objects such as toys, but here we're using it to patch and fill holes.

Wool fibres are covered in tiny scales that lock together when poked with a felting needle. It's a little bit magic and a great technique for beginners because it's easier and faster than darning. In my mending course, students learn darning before needle felting for one important reason: if I taught needle felting first, that's all they'd want to do!

I call it 'the blues buster'; it's exciting and calming simultaneously. It appeals to my fun and creative side, and it's satisfyingly repetitive – perfect for achieving maximum mendfulness.

Thank you to Heleen Klopper of Woolfiller for discovering the wonderful mending potential of this technique.

COCONUT
TEA

THE ESSENTIALS

Clothing or blankets in need of TLC. Needle felting works best on knitwear and blankets made from animal fibres – wool, cashmere, etc. – but feel free to experimend. It's great for cashmere and thin woollen knitwear where darning would be more time-consuming and eye-straining. But darning is stronger and the best method for socks and other items that experience a lot of wear and tear. Hand-knitted clothing is better suited to darning, aesthetically speaking, but it can also be needle felted.

Table or sturdy work surface; this is not a lap project – there are sharp needles involved!

Felting needle(s), unlike sewing needles, these have special notches or barbs that help fibres bind together; 38-gauge is a good all-purpose size for this task.

Felting surface: high-density foam block OR hessian/burlap bag filled with rice are perfect for felting. If using foam, it needs to provide adequate resistance to protect your needle and work surface. Upholstery foam works well; check your local foam-and-rubber store for offcuts that would otherwise go to landfill. Use a foam stress ball for small areas (e.g. sleeves), or cut a piece of foam to size. (Stretching a garment to fit a too-large piece of foam will give you poor results.) A more environmentally friendly alternative to foam is the hessian/burlap bag filled with rice, which can be composted at the end of its useful life. Make one from an empty coffee sack for bonus enviro-points!

Wool fleece is puffy, fluffy wool that has been scoured (cleaned) but not spun into yarn. It resembles candy floss (cotton candy) and takes a variety of forms and names – look for roving, wool batts/batting, tops or slivers. Most fluffy animal fibres will work: wool, alpaca, cashmere... even fluffy cat fur! Vegan fleece – made from acrylic or plant fibres such as bamboo or tencel – is available but more difficult to find. You can also use fuzz collected from wool or cashmere knitwear (see the method on page 132).

OPTIONAL EXTRAS

Biscuit/cookie cutters or a fabric-marking tool for drawing a design. Biscuit cutters can be used as templates for simple shapes but they can also tempt you to pack in too much fleece. A water-erasable marker will give you the neatest result, but if your garment is dark or highly textured this will be challenging. I've successfully made templates from cereal-box cardboard – I cut my desired shape out of cardboard, begin felting with the template in place, then remove it as soon as possible for fine-tuning.

Fabric comb (sweater comb) for removing fuzz from clothing to use for invisible mending (see page 132).

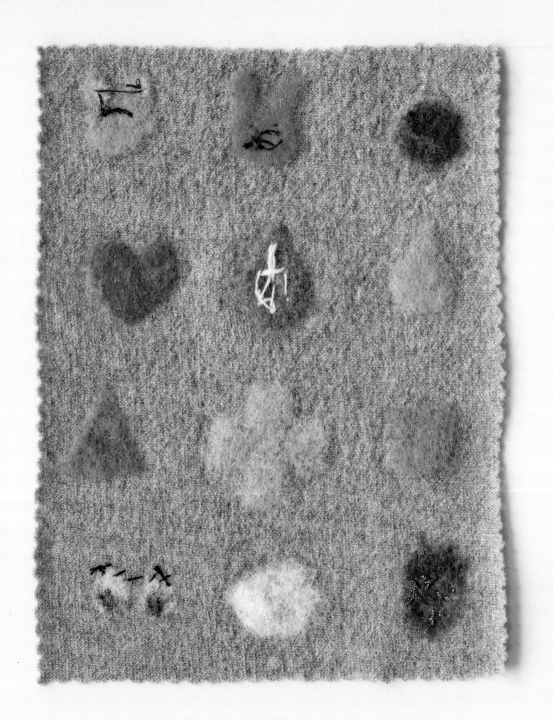

BACK

FRONT

6a

SAFETY WARNING: Please be careful; needle felting is genuinely so much fun that it's easy to stop paying attention to what you're doing and stab yourself.

1. Make a cup of tea for maximum mendfulness. Needle felting is quick so you only need a cup!

2. Decide which side of your garment to work on (inside-out or right side around). For crisp, well-defined edges, work from the right side. For a softer look, work inside-out.

3. Choose a basic shape to cover the hole(s). Dots are the easiest and great for covering multiple holes but can look lonely on their own or as a pair. Swiss crosses look like cute first-aid symbols, and hearts are fun if you're mending something for a friend. The fewer and larger the angles, the easier the shape is to make.

4. Insert the felting surface inside or underneath your garment, directly under the hole. Optional: place a biscuit cutter over the hole as a guide or use a fabric-marking tool to draw an outline of your design.

6b

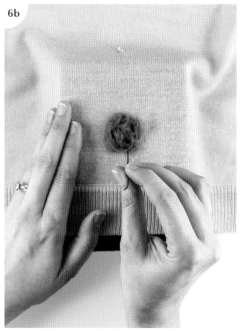

7

5. Place a small piece of fleece over the hole. You want just enough fleece to cover the hole completely and add a border of 5mm (¼in) or more. (If you're using a biscuit cutter, avoid the temptation to pack it full of fleece or you will be felting forever. You can add more as you go.) You should now have a craft sandwich: felting surface on the bottom, your garment in the middle and fleece (in biscuit cutter, if using) on top.

6. Holding the needle between your thumb and first two fingers, poke through all the layers of the sandwich, only just poking through the felting surface. Lift the needle and repeat, working from the centre outwards, until the hole is securely covered.

7. Every so often, gently lift your garment off the felting surface and reposition it. Pull carefully to avoid damaging your work or felting surface. You can also use this opportunity to check the other side and make sure your hole is completely covered.

→

9a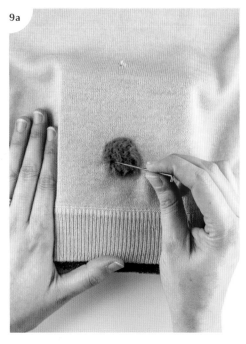

9b

←

8. Once the centre is securely felted, tidy up the edges. Fold any stray fuzz back in toward the centre and gently poke it in place.

9. If you like, you can add more wool and keep building on your design. You can make the patch larger if your hole is still visible, cover up any thin spots, even out designs that aren't symmetrical and/or add different colours. Keep going until the design is flat and fully matted. (If you've used too much fleece it won't ever flatten completely; you can either accept the puffiness or remove it and start again.)

10. Optional: for a more finished look, trim any straggly fibres with small, sharp scissors and apply a steam iron for a few seconds to make the patch flat and smooth. If you like, you can embellish your work with embroidery (see Stitching section, page 38, for instructions).

PRO TIPS

o Buy fleece in colours that make your heart sing because a little goes a long way and it will last for ages.

o You can mix colours before you felt to get a better colour match. Dani Ives's book *Painting with Wool* covers colour blending in detail.

o For faster felting try holding two needles at the same time.

o For the most professional, I-bought-it-this-way look, make your mends a consistent shape and size throughout the garment (particularly dots), but feel free to mix it up with different colours.

o If you're mending a large hole, you can add additional fleece to the reverse side to help plug the hole so your patch doesn't sink in. Flip the garment occasionally and felt from each side.

o Hand-wash needle-felted garments for best results, and dry flat on a clothes rack or towel to avoid shrinkage.

EXPERIMEND

I've used wool here because it's commercially available, comes in gorgeous colours and is ready to use. But other animal fibres could work – alpaca, rabbit, long-haired cat or dog fur – as long as the fibres are long, fluffy and clean. (Wash them gently to avoid felting before you're ready, and only collect fibres for the purpose of fur and coat maintenance. For inspiration, read *Crafting with Cat Hair*.) Vegan fleeces are also commercially available but harder to find – head to Resources (page 262) for a list of suppliers. I've had surprising success with acrylic fleece.

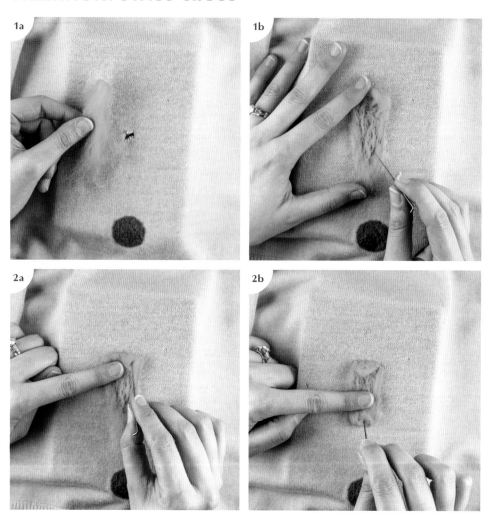

1. Needle-felt a long, skinny piece of fleece over your hole, starting from the centre and working outward, until it's secure but not fully felted.

2. Fold the fleece back on itself at each end and poke it in place to make crisp edges. You can gently drag out fibres with your needle to make nice corners.

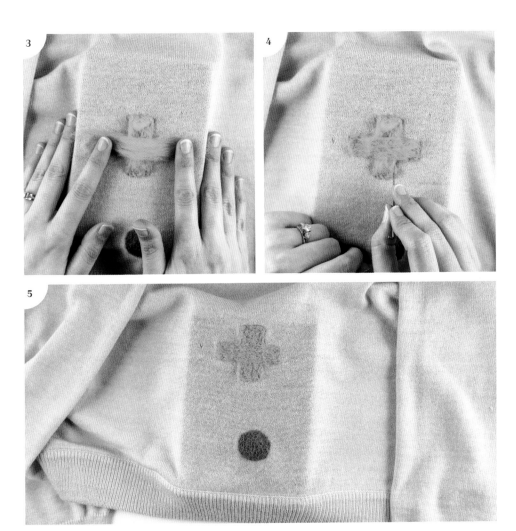

3. Before you perfect your first rectangle, add another long, skinny piece of fleece on top and repeat steps 1 and 2. Working with two partially felted rectangles gives you more flexibility when you're trying to make your cross symmetrical (the trickiest part of the process).

4. Continue to felt and add more wool until you're happy with the shape and it's symmetrical.

5. Continue felting until your design is flat and fully matted.

METHOD: INVISIBLE MENDING
WITH FUZZ FROM YOUR GARMENT

This works best with cashmere and soft woollen knitwear.

1. Using a fabric comb, gently remove fuzz from the garment you're mending.

2. Pull apart any pill fuzz with your fingernails until it's a feltable candy-floss/cotton-candy texture. (Pilling is a form of felting; if you skip this step your mend might look more like popcorn than smooth felt.)

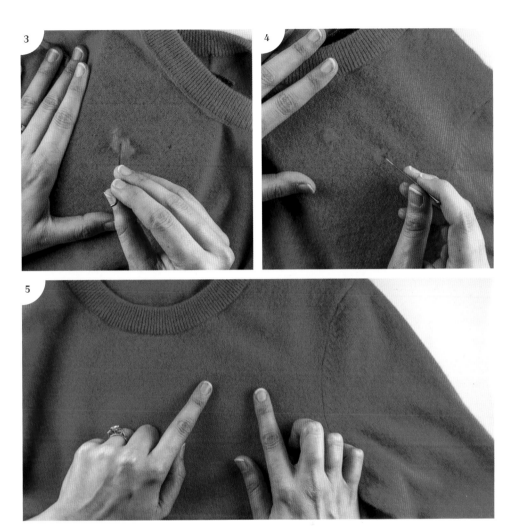

3. Working inside-out for maximum invisibility, insert the felting surface underneath the hole and poke the fuzz in place.

4. Occasionally flip the garment right side out and poke the fuzzy fibres in the other direction.

5. Keep going until you are happy with the result and the fleece is flat and fully integrated.

1

3

1. Place a medium piece of fleece directly onto your felting surface.

2. Poke the fleece with the needle repeatedly to flatten it.

3. Occasionally lift the flattened fleece patch off of the felting surface and flip it like a pancake to ensure even felting from both sides.

4. If you'll be sewing your patch in place, keep poking until the patch is felted completely and add more wool to any thin areas – it should be opaque when you hold it up to the light. If you're only semi-felting, you can stop a bit earlier and then finish the felting process when you attach the patch to the item you're mending.

4

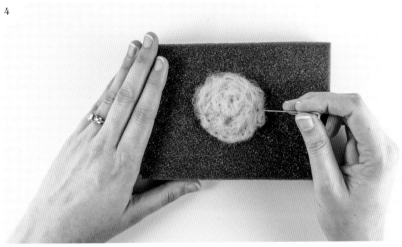

6a

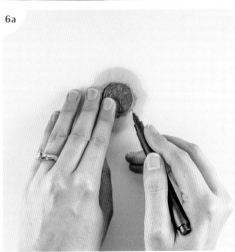

6b

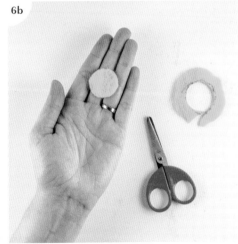

5. For best results, apply a steam iron for a few seconds to make the patch flat and smooth.

6. Cut out your desired shape(s) from the flat patch. You can cut freehand or trace a coin or biscuit cutter as your guide.

7. Attach the patch to the item you're mending, with the felting needle or with a sewing needle and thread.

What could go wrong?

Ouch! I accidentally stabbed my finger with the needle.

It happens. Just go slowly and take extra care when moving the needle near your fingers.

I broke my needle.

Needles can break for a number of reasons, including using too much force, but often it's a mystery. One broken needle is too small and sharp to be recycled or binned on its own safely; humans collect and sort our rubbish and recycling and you don't want them to get stuck accidentally. Many sewists and menders collect their broken needles and pins in an old tin or jar and, once it's full, seal and dispose of the whole thing or empty it into a sharps container (you can find one at a pharmacy, a local health clinic or a doctor's office – check your local council or government websites for locations close to you). If you find you're breaking needles repeatedly, try altering your felting technique by adjusting your speed and how you hold the needle.

My design is too puffy.

If you're using a biscuit cutter, avoid the temptation to pack it with fleece or you will be felting forever. You can always add more as you go. If the biscuit cutter isn't helpful, try cutting your desired shape out of cereal-box cardboard or a business card to use as a template; a flat template won't trick you into over-stuffing your design. Or – if the garment you're mending is pale in colour – try using a water-erasable or air-erasable fabric marker to trace your design (see Kate's cardigan, page 218).

I can see holes in my wool.

That's normal. Finer needles make smaller holes but increase felting time. Holes will usually disappear if you iron your finished piece with a steam iron.

The fleece won't stick to my garment.

This is more likely to happen when your fleece or the item you're mending is made from synthetic or plant fibres (e.g. cotton) instead of animal fibres, but occasionally I experience it with wool fleece on wool clothing. Garments made from 'superwash' wool have had their feltable scales removed or coated intentionally to prevent shrinkage when washing. Smooth fibres are more resistant to needle felting because there's nothing for the needle to grab onto and felt together. Having said that, though, I am continually learning and surprised by what will and won't work with this technique. Sometimes I think a particular fabric is totally unsuitable for needle felting so I don't recommend it, then my students ignore me and make it work (successful surprises include a pair of jeans, a damask tablecloth, gym gear, and 100% acrylic fleece). So experimend and see what happens! If needle felting directly onto your garment isn't working, you can pre-felt a patch first (see page 134 for details), then sew it to your garment with needle and thread (see Erin's shirt, page 206).

My needle-felting is not symmetrical.

Keep adding small bits of wool to build your design until it's how you like it. Sometimes adjusting your speed can help, too – I tend to peck at the wool slowly and carefully around the edges to make sure it looks how I want it, and poke quickly when I'm flattening my design.

My design has puffy edges.

I call this the 'pizza crust' effect. You shouldn't be able to lift and wiggle the edges of your design – they should be flat and fully integrated into the item you're mending. For perfect crustless edges, poke slowly and deliberately around the border, sometimes at a 45-degree angle, until the fleece is fully flattened. The pace of this motion is more like marching rather than walking or running – slow, regular and considered. ✕

TECHNIQUE:

machine darning

Visible mending is awesome... except for when attracting attention to a particular area is the last thing you want to do.

Most clothing can be mended well by hand. But this is the strongest and least visible method for mending jeans, and 'HELP! How do I mend this hole in the crotch/thigh/bum of my jeans?' is the question I get asked most often.

Professional jeans menders often use specialty darning machines, but you can get a decent result with a standard home sewing machine. I've outlined two different methods here:

o   **Free-motion darning**, where you stitch freely in any direction, is safer because you can control the fabric with both hands. It's different to standard sewing so it can take a bit of getting used to, but it's also pretty fun, and thrilling once you realize what your machine can do. Not all sewing machines can free-motion stitch; see 'What you need' for details.

o   **Straight-stitch darning** works on most sewing machines but is trickier than free-motion darning – at times you'll need to move the fabric through your machine with only one hand.

I prefer straight-stitch darning because I'm confident with my machine and often too lazy to change its settings – I like to move quickly through my mending pile once I'm in the mood. My students tend to prefer free-motion darning because it's unusual, fun and easier to control.

If you don't have sewing-machine experience but really want to give machine darning a try, ask a friend or family member to give you a lesson first, or enrol in a sewing course. If you don't have access to a sewing machine, try patching or darning by hand instead.

THE ESSENTIALS

Sewing-machine confidence (not pictured). This is not a first-timer's project! Machine darning is a billion times safer, easier and more fun if you are somewhat comfortable using a sewing machine; even more so if it's a machine you know well. My students are often shocked by the difference between a machine they've used before and the machine they use in class, particularly when it comes to speed.

Trousers or another garment with rips, holes or threadbare areas. Machine darning works best on sturdy woven fabrics like denim, canvas, cotton twill and linen; it's not suitable for delicate or stretch-knit fabrics, although I've had good results with stretch denim (just take extra care not to stretch or tug on the fabric while you stitch).

Sewing machine:

o   For free-motion darning you'll need a machine that can disable its 'feed dogs' (the metal teeth that guide fabric when you sew). Some machines have a lever that lowers the feed dogs; mine has a special plate that covers them. Check your sewing-machine manual if you're unsure. And you'll need a darning foot (AKA a free-motion embroidery foot or free-motion quilting foot); mine was an optional accessory for my machine that I purchased separately. It is possible to free-motion stitch without a darning foot but you're more likely to bend or break the needle, have problems with thread tension or get your fingers in the way (ouch!). If you try free-motion darning without a darning foot, make sure to lower your presser bar (as if you have a foot installed) before you start stitching.

o   For straight-stitch darning almost any home sewing machine is suitable, as long as it has a reverse-stitch function (antique and industrial machines often don't). If not, you can try the pivot method (see page 152) or borrow someone else's machine for this task.

Sewing thread – you'll need all-purpose thread for the needle and the bobbin, and, optionally, thread for restitching any seams you might need to unpick. For best results, use good-quality thread for this task. The two secrets to well-blended machine darning are to stitch with the grainline or weave pattern of your fabric (see Fabric 101 on page 26) – whichever is more noticeable – and to select thread colours that match what you're mending. Denim is usually woven from white weft threads and dark warp threads, but the most invisible match might be a colour (or colours) somewhere in between the two.

→

WHAT YOU NEED

Well-loved denim will feature a range of shades, thanks to fading and wear over time; choose what blends best with the spot you'll be mending.

- ○ **All-purpose sewing thread** is usually made from polyester, cotton or a mixture. For a blended mend choose a colour or colours to match your garment. The bobbin-thread colour is less important (if your tension is correct it won't be visible).

- ○ **Topstitching thread** is thicker and good for decorative stitching on jeans pockets, side seams and hems. When using topstitching thread, use all-purpose sewing thread in the bobbin. Some sewing machines struggle with topstitching tension; you can get a similar look with all-purpose sewing thread and a triple straight stitch (which looks like this: |||).

Sewing-machine needle of the right type and size for the fabric you're mending, e.g. a jeans needle or large universal needle (size 90/14 or 100/16) for denim. A new, sharp needle is best – not a dull one you've used a few times.

Fabric scrap for test stitching, similar in weight and feel to what you're mending.

A sharp pair of scissors for trimming excess threads and fabric.

If you're mending a hole or rip large enough to poke your finger through (not just a thinning, threadbare area), you will need a few extra things:

- ○ **Fabric scrap** for reinforcement. For a blended mend with more stitching (which adds stiffness), thin, soft fabric is best. If your garment is loose-fitting or you're only darning lightly, you can use thicker fabric scraps.

- ○ **Hand-sewing needle and thread** for tacking/basting your patch to your garment. Machine darning is often used on areas that are awkward to sew; tacking/basting means you won't have to worry about pins or safety pins, which keeps your fingers safer. I like to tack/baste patch edges in a contrasting colour so it's easy to see and remove, but I prefer matching thread for the edges of a hole – if the stitches are difficult to remove once you've stitched over them with the machine, at least they won't be visible.

OPTIONAL EXTRAS

Seam ripper for unpicking seams and any stitching mistakes.

Embroidery hoop for free-motion darning. An embroidery hoop works as a steering wheel. Ideally, the hoop should be larger than the area you're mending; 20cm (8in) is a good size. Most embroidery hoops are too thick to fit in my machine, so I use a slimmer spring-tension embroidery hoop when machine darning.

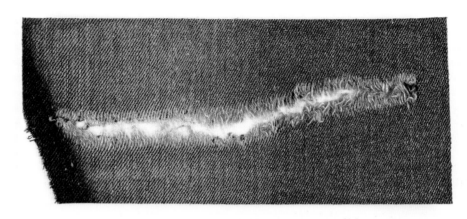

BEFORE

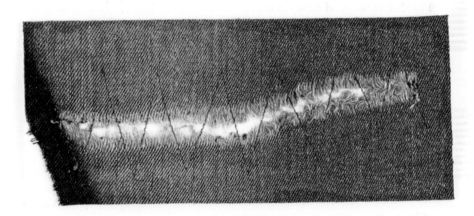

FIRST PASS

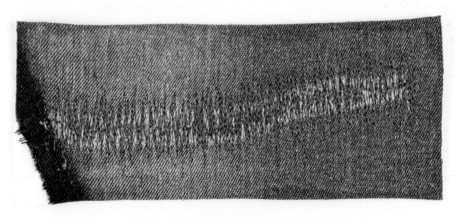

SIXTH PASS

1. Make a cup of tea. If you are nervous about trying a new technique, a relaxing cup of tea can help calm the nerves.

2. Assess the damage to be mended and trim any loose, straggly threads so they won't get caught up in your machine. (Trust me on this. If you ignore my advice and get stuck, I won't hear you calling for help!)

3. If the damage is next to or underneath a seam, pocket or belt loop, use your seam ripper to unpick the stitching in that area for best results and easier handling (you can restitch it later).

4b

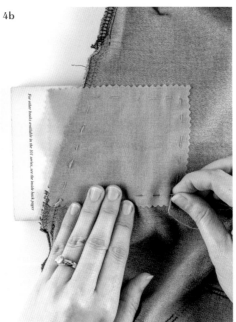

4c

4. If you're mending a full-blown hole or rip, you'll need a patch:

    a. Cut a fabric patch much larger than the damaged area (you'll trim the excess later).

    b. Turn your garment inside-out and tack/baste the patch in place around the border. (To help prevent sewing trousers shut by mistake, you can slip a book or piece of cardboard inside the trouser leg while you stitch.)

    c. Turn the garment right side out. Tack/baste along the edges of any big holes or rips to keep them from getting caught in your machine.

    d. If you've unpicked stitching on a feature like a pocket or belt loop to get better access, you can peel back the feature and stitch it down (temporarily) so it's out of your way for the next part.

5. Set aside your cup of tea for the moment because we're heading to the sewing machine next, and electrical appliances and hot liquids don't mix!

4

SAFETY WARNING: To avoid stitching through your fingers, keep your hands on the embroidery hoop, not the fabric, and turn off your machine if you need to move your fingers near the needle, e.g. to remove caught threads.

1. Disable your sewing machine's feed dogs and install the darning foot as per your instruction manual.

2. Lift the presser foot and thread the needle and bobbin threads through your machine.

3. Select the straight-stitch option on your machine and set your stitch length to zero (some machines do this automatically when you disable the feed dogs). Your actual stitch length will be determined by how you move your fabric (magic!).

4. Test your thread tension. Some machines set the tension automatically when you disable the feed dogs; if not, adjust it yourself. Insert your test fabric scrap into the machine and lower the presser foot. Practise stitching (in any direction),

then stop and determine whether your stitching is too tight, too loose or just right – your test stitches should be even, look the same on the right side and wrong side and not have any noticeable loops or knots. For best results, stitch at a high speed while moving the fabric gently at a slow-to-moderate speed (the slow movements will seem strange at first compared to normal sewing). I find that the harder I push and pull the fabric, the more it resists – slow and steady wins the race! A low tension setting (1 or 2) is usually preferred for free-motion stitching but your optimum tension setting will vary depending on the fabric and thread you're using and how you move the fabric through the machine. If you need to adjust your tension, lift your presser foot and change the setting one number at a time before lowering your presser foot and stitching again. Repeat as necessary. If you're not sure how to adjust your tension settings, check your machine's instruction manual.

5. Once your tension is correct, you can test any other thread colours you're considering and practise your technique to get comfortable with free-motion stitching. Once you're finished, remove the test scrap from the machine.

6. Frame the area to be mended in an embroidery hoop, if you're using one. Unlike hand stitching, where the fabric rests on top of the hoop, with machine darning you want your fabric to sit at the bottom of the hoop so it touches the base of your machine. Make sure only one layer of fabric is in the hoop so you don't sew your trouser legs or pockets shut.

7. Lift the presser foot and place your hooped garment at the base of the machine. Clear away any fabric layers you don't want to sew through (e.g. pockets). Lower the presser foot.

→

8

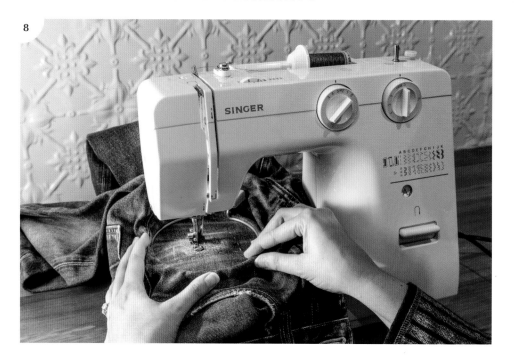

←

8. Get into a comfortable position and grab the hoop with both hands. Make a few stitches, reverse (backstitch) for a few stitches to secure your threads, then stop and trim your thread ends. Begin stitching in any direction over the damaged area, using your hands to steer the hooped fabric. For a blended mend, follow the grainline or weave pattern of your fabric. For a fun mend you can doodle as you would with a pen or pencil. Keep stitching until you are happy with the coverage, but don't stitch more than necessary or you will make your garment too stiff. If you are only lightly darning: once you're finished, reverse (backstitch) for a few stitches, then forward a few stitches, to secure your threads. (If the darned area is densely stitched, you can skip this step because you're essentially backstitching already.)

9. Remove your garment from the machine, then remove the embroidery hoop.

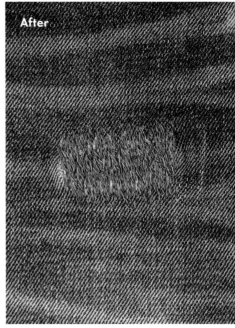

10. Snip off the loose thread ends and unpick any tacking/basting stitches. Trim any excess patch fabric. (For bonus enviro-points, save your scraps to use as stuffing for another project.)

11. Once you're happy with your mend, you can restitch any seams you unpicked earlier. Set your machine back to standard straight stitching: re-enable your feed dogs, switch to a standard sewing foot, increase your stitch length and adjust your thread tension for the thread you'll be using. Don't rely on the tension setting you normally use for sewing projects; different tension settings are needed when you're using topstitching thread and/or sewing through multiple layers of sturdy fabric. You can practise on your fabric scrap – fold it in half so that it resembles what you'll be restitching.

→

SAFETY WARNING: Driving with one hand can be dangerous. To avoid stitching through your fingers, make sure to go slowly and turn off your machine if you need to move your fingers near the needle, e.g. to remove caught threads. If you can adjust the speed on your machine, use the slowest setting. If your machine is operated by a foot pedal, put as little pressure on it as possible; imagine you are a tiny mouse stepping on the pedal.

1. Select the straight-stitch option on your machine and choose your preferred stitch length. Smaller stitches blend in better but are harder to unpick if you make a mistake. I usually set my stitch length to around 2 or 3mm for this method.

2. Lift the presser foot and thread the needle and bobbin threads through the machine.

3. Test your thread tension. Thread tension ranges from 0 to 9 and the standard default tension setting for straight stitching is usually 4.5, but this can change over time if your machine hasn't been serviced in a while, and your optimum tension setting will vary from project to project, depending on the thread and fabric you're using. Insert your test fabric scrap into the machine and lower the presser foot. Practise stitching straight lines, then stop and determine whether your stitching is too tight, too loose or just right – your test stitches should be even, look the same on top and bottom and not have any noticeable loops or knots. If you need to adjust your tension, lift your presser foot and change the setting one number at a time

before lowering your presser foot and stitching again. Repeat as necessary. If you're not sure how to adjust your tension settings, check your instruction manual.

4. Once your tension is correct, you can test any other thread colours you're considering. When you're finished, remove the test scrap from the machine.

5. Lift the presser foot and place your garment at the base of the machine, with the needle positioned top left of the damaged area. Make sure only one layer of fabric is positioned under the needle (move pockets out of the way) so you don't sew your trouser legs or pockets shut.

→

6a

←

6. Start from the top-left corner and make a few stitches. Reverse (backstitch) for a few stitches to secure your threads, then stitch down in a straight line, following the grainline or weave pattern of your fabric. Now you have two options:

   a. **One-handed driving:** Hold the reverse-stitch button or lever with one hand and reverse stitch at a slight angle, gently steering the fabric with your other hand. You'll have an easier time if you work with your machine – your feed dogs will guide the fabric in a straight line; you just need to keep it on course.

   b. **Pivot (never look back):** If you're able to turn your garment 180 degrees, you can pivot – a sewing method that allows you to change the direction of your stitches while still sewing forward. To pivot: lower your needle fully so it's piercing your fabric, lift your presser foot, turn (AKA pivot) your fabric to the desired position, lower your presser foot and resume stitching.

7. SLOWLY sew forward and backward over the damage. Start by working your way left to right, with wider zigzags on your first pass (to ensure rip edges are securely held down), then move back right to left and fill in the details. Try to stagger the edges of your stitching to prevent further rips in this area.

8. Repeat until you're happy with the coverage and it blends in, but don't stitch more than necessary or you will make your garment too stiff. If you are only lightly darning the damaged area, once you're

finished, reverse (backstitch) for a few stitches, then forward a few stitches, to secure your threads. (If the darned area is densely stitched, skip this step because you're essentially backstitching already.)

9. Remove your garment from the sewing machine.

10. Snip off the loose thread ends and unpick any visible tacking/basting stitches. Trim any excess patch fabric. For bonus enviro-points, save your scraps to use as stuffing for another project.

→

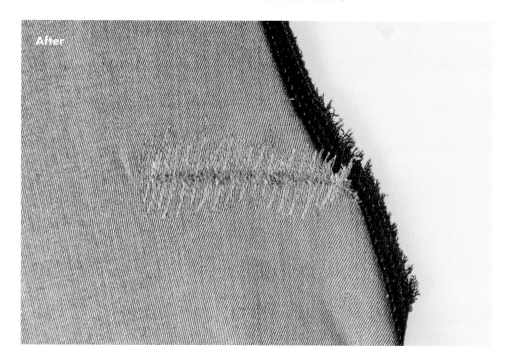

After

←

11. Once you're happy with your mend, you can restitch any seams you unpicked earlier. You might need to adjust your thread tension and stitch length. Don't rely on the tension setting you normally use for sewing projects; different tension settings are needed when you're using topstitching thread and/or sewing through multiple layers of sturdy fabric. You can practise on your fabric scrap – fold it in half to make it bulkier and resemble more closely what you'll be restitching.

PRO TIPS

o   Mend or reinforce your clothes
    at the first sign of damage.
    A stitch in time really does save
    nine – a threadbare area is much
    easier and quicker to repair than a
    full-blown rip or hole.

o   Use a new needle and good-
    quality thread in your machine
    for this task. 'Mystery thread' –
    anything old, second-hand or of
    dubious quality – might be fine for
    hand sewing, but it's less reliable
    in a sewing machine and more
    prone to breakage. Signs of poor
    quality include fluffiness (thread
    that is not tightly spun when
    inspected up close), lack of visible
    branding, and if it was purchased
    from a discount shop.

o   Sewing machine instruction
    manuals are incredibly useful;
    if you can't find yours, try
    searching online for a copy.
    I keep mine in my sewing
    machine case so it's easy to
    find when I need it.

o   Use a bit of liquid seam sealant
    to seal any worn spots you can't
    sew over easily (e.g. hems and
    pocket edges) – it will make your
    clothes last longer.

EXPERIMENT

For visible mending use a
contrasting colour thread,
or add a colourful patch
underneath the hole and
darn lightly so the new
fabric becomes a feature.

For free-motion darning,
try 'drawing' images or
words with thread. For
next-level free-motion
stitching inspiration, see
Organic Embroidery by
Meredith Woolnough.

What could go wrong?

I've sewn through my finger!

Ouch! I've seen this happen a couple of times and it's usually the result of one or more factors:

1. Lack of sewing-machine confidence (this is not the time to fake it till you make it).
2. Sewing too fast and giving yourself a fright in the process.
3. Accidentally pressing the foot pedal while your fingers are near the needle (to remove caught threads or pins).

Safety first: when straight-stitch darning, sew as slowly as possible and turn off your machine if you need to get near the needle. If you get stressed (which can affect your capacity to make good decisions), take some time out with a cup of tea to calm down before you try again.

My trousers are too skinny and difficult to move around on the sewing machine.

The easiest option is to unpick a side seam before you start, which will give you a flatter piece of fabric to manoeuvre. Another option for knee holes is to sew with the weft threads, following the line of the rip rather than stitching across it.

I broke my needle.

One broken needle is too small and sharp to be recycled or binned on its own safely; humans collect and sort our rubbish and recycling and you don't want them to get stuck accidentally. Many sewists and menders collect their broken needles and pins in an old tin or jar and, once it's full, seal and dispose of the whole thing or empty it into a sharps container (you can find one at a pharmacy, a local health clinic or a doctor's office – check your local council or government websites for locations close to you). To prevent breakages, replace sewing-machine needles regularly and make sure you're using the correct type and size for the fabric you're stitching.

My thread keeps breaking.

Check that your needle and bobbin are threaded correctly and rethread if necessary. Make sure you're using good-quality thread in your machine; old thread and cheaply made thread are more prone to breakage.

My thread is not blending in.

Try blending two or more colours to get a more natural result. Following the grainline or weave pattern of your fabric with your stitching will help you get a better result, too.

I made a tangled mess of threads.

Make sure to always lower your presser foot before you start stitching. If that's not the culprit, you can try rethreading the machine, checking the bobbin case to make sure it's threaded properly or testing your thread tension.

My sewing machine hates me and is not cooperating.

When was the last time you cleaned your machine and oiled it, or had it professionally serviced? If the answer is 'never' or 'I don't remember',

it's time! Your machine prefers a dust-free, well-lubricated environment. Manufacturers often recommend that you get your machine professionally serviced every 12–18 months, or sooner if you notice any changes or unusual noises. If you're not confident troubleshooting on your machine, ask a sewist friend to assist or sign up for a refresher sewing course. I attended a sewing-machine-maintenance course and found it incredibly helpful.

I mended my jeans but new holes keep appearing!

This is frustrating but totally normal, especially if the damage is due to frequent rubbing (hello, thighs!), frequent activity (hello, cyclists!) or someone stubbornly wearing trousers that are too tight and hulking out of them (speaking from experience). For best results mend early – preventatively, if you can – rather than wait for a full-blown hole or rip to appear. In future try to buy jeans made from thicker denim – 100% cotton if possible. The thinner the fabric and the higher the synthetic content (e.g. lycra/spandex/elastane), the more quickly they'll wear out. ✕

EXTRAS:

buttons

Sewing on a button has to be one of the quickest, easiest fixes. People often confess to me that they don't know the 'right' way to sew on a button, but – spoiler alert! – there's no one right way to do it, so long as it's secure and the threads aren't loose. Here I show you the process of how I like to do it.

There are two main types of buttons: flat (pictured) and shank. The steps for sewing a shank button are similar, only you're sewing through one hole at the back of the button instead.

Four-hole buttons can be stitched in so many ways. You can even create letters: C, L, N, O, U, X and Z (the next time buttons pop off a pair of pyjamas in my house, you can bet I'll be stitching ZZZ through the buttons' holes). When you need to replace a button, why not try a different button colour, thread colour or stitch pattern and make it a feature?

If a button has ripped through your garment and created a hole (a common occurrence with shirt buttons), remove the button, patch the fabric to reinforce it, then reattach the button.

To repair a damaged buttonhole, use the tailor's buttonhole stitch (page 50).

METHOD: FLAT BUTTON

1. Thread your needle and knot the thread. For a longer-lasting hold, use heavy-duty or topstitching thread, double the thread before you knot it, and/or use beeswax.

2. Make a stitch or two in the fabric. I like to place my knot on the right side of the fabric if I'm sewing a large button, as the button will hide the knot, but it doesn't matter which side you choose.

3. Poke your needle up through one hole and down through another.

4. Before you finish the first stitch, place a match or toothpick between the button and fabric. This creates a gap to prevent overly tight stitches – essential for coats and other thick garments. Then stitch down through the fabric near where you first came up. Keep stitching – two or three times around for each set of holes – until the button is secure.

5. Remove the match or toothpick and pull the button up from the fabric.

6. For added strength, bring your needle and thread up between the fabric and the button, and wrap your thread clockwise around the stitched button threads a few times. Once you've finished wrapping your threads, stitch through to the back and make a knot.

2

3

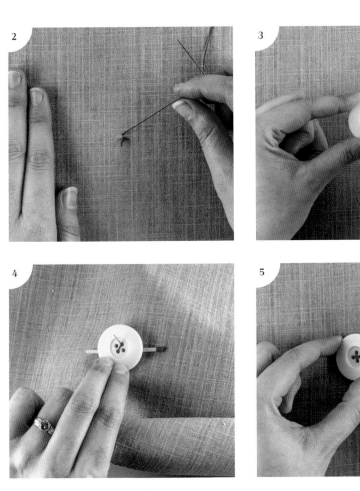

4

5

6a

6b

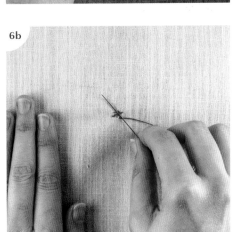

EXTRAS:

zippers

Zippers are like snakes to me and I will do anything to avoid fixing them. There's little creativity involved, just persistence. On the plus side, zipper troubleshooting and repairs are pretty straightforward, and when you fix one you will feel like a total champion.

There are a few different types of zippers but only two options when they break: repair or replace.

Zipper deal-breakers (problems requiring full replacement) include:

o   Missing or damaged teeth
o   Damaged tape
o   Missing or damaged box on a separating zipper (found in jackets and sleeping bags)
o   Zipper won't close because your trousers or shoes are too tight (zippers wear out if there's too much pressure on them).

Zipper replacement is a whole other world with different methods for jackets, trousers, bags, etc. If you aren't up for the challenge, support your local alterations shop, or if you'd like to DIY, *The Sewing Bible for Clothes Alterations* by Judith Turner is a good place to start.

The potentially fixable problems often can be solved with a bar of soap or beeswax, a pair of pliers and/or use of swear words. You can buy replacement parts (see Resources, page 262), or try transplanting parts from an old metal zipper in a similar size and style (charity/thrift shops are overflowing with them).

ZIPPER HALL OF SHAME

DAMAGED SLIDER

MISALIGNMENT

ALL THE THINGS: MISALIGNMENT, MISSING TEETH AND MISSING BOX

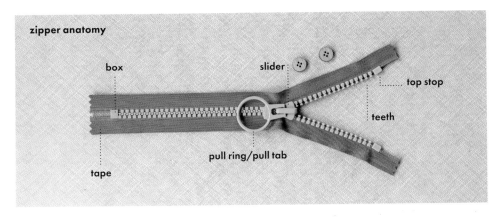

zipper anatomy

box

slider

top stop

teeth

pull ring/pull tab

tape

REPAIR

Common fixable problems:

o **Slider is stuck or doesn't align teeth properly.** Rub a bar of soap or beeswax on the zipper teeth, then jiggle the slider back and forth. Repeat as necessary. If the teeth are misaligned, you can try using a paperclip or pen to pry open the teeth near where the misalignment begins and try the soapy jiggle as above. Check that there's not a damaged or missing tooth, which means full replacement is required.

o **Missing pull tab or pull ring.** If the loop where the pull tab attaches is still intact, replace the pull tab with a paper clip, keyring, or leather cord.

o **Missing/damaged/loose slider.** Replace the slider. Sliders come in many sizes and styles; if you don't have the original, make sure the replacement is similar (some have a code on the back for identification). You might need to temporarily remove the top stops with pliers to attach the slider (possible with metal zips but not plastic ones), or try rubbing soap or beeswax on the top stops and first few teeth and tugging. If you've attached the slider but it's loose and doesn't stay attached, you can crimp it together (gently) with a pair of pliers to tighten it. If the slider has fallen off a separating zipper (commonly found on jackets and coats) because the box is missing, you will need to replace the entire zipper.

o **Missing top stop**. Replace the top stop. You can transplant a metal stop from another zipper with pliers, but plastic stops are not transplantable.

o **Missing or damaged box.** If the zipper is meant to be permanently closed at one end (known as a non-separating zipper), create a new end point by making multiple satin stitches by hand in the same spot (a neat sewing trick for shortening zippers, too). If it's a separating zipper, you'll need a full replacement.

o **Trouser zipper slides down and won't stay shut**. Attach a keyring to the pull tab and hang it on the top button before buttoning up your trousers.

ladders

Ladders, found in knit fabrics, might look complicated but they're easy and fun to fix once you get started. A ladder (also known as a run, or dropped stitches) occurs when a knit stitch is damaged and drops the stitches below it, setting off a chain reaction. To prevent a ladder from getting worse, hold the last intact stitch in place with a safety pin until you have time to mend it.

To fix a ladder, you'll need a crochet hook or small latch hook – see page 21 in Tools of the Trade for details. Hooks come in different sizes; choose one to suit the thickness of the yarn you're mending.

Fixing ladders on thin, machine-knitted clothing can be eye-straining and more trouble than it's worth so I'll usually darn instead, but if I can easily see the surrounding knit stitches without squinting, I will jump at the chance to fix a ladder because it's so quick and satisfying.

If your ladder is next to a hole, fix the ladder first, as it could shrink the hole and reduce your mending time.

METHOD

1. With the right side of the garment in front of you (the pattern of Vs should be visible), poke your hook through the last intact knit stitch as shown.

2. While your hook is inserted into the stitch, pick up the dropped stitch above it.

3. Pull the dropped stitch through the loop upwards.

4. Repeat until you get to the end of the ladder.

5. This last step will depend on what's at the end of your ladder. If you've closed up all the gaps and there is no hole, stitch down the top of the ladder with matching yarn or sewing thread to secure it. If there's a hole at the end of your ladder, secure the top of the ladder with a safety pin or thread, then darn the hole.

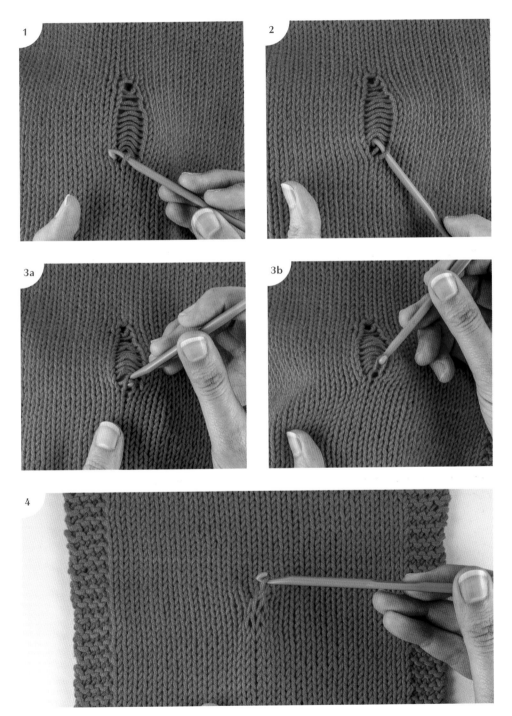

snags

If you have pets or jewellery that snag your clothing or furniture, this one's for you.

For hand-knitted and reversible garments, it's worth trying to ease snagged yarn back in place, gently, but for most modern clothing, it's nearly impossible so your best option is to hide the snag instead.

I've shown two methods here, using two different types of needles:

o   A **snag repair needle** has a rough-textured end, similar to a metal file, that grabs snagged threads and pulls them through to the other side of fabric. It's the quicker and easier method for this technique – a time-saver if you often have snags to deal with – but you don't need one. The snag repair needle's rough texture could damage delicate fabric, so use the sewing-needle method if you're repairing silk or other delicate fabrics.

o   A **basic hand-sewing needle** can be used to fix snags if the eye is large enough to accommodate the snagged thread. A needle threader would make this method trickier, so select a needle you can thread without one. This technique is also useful for darning, for when you need to weave in too-short yarn ends.

When you're finished you can leave the hidden snag as is (no knots required, and snipping could cause further damage); no one will see it because it's on the inside of your garment. A steam iron can help smooth out any minor puckering.

To fix snags on furniture, enter and exit the fabric horizontally with your needle in one motion, as if you're loading your needle for running stitch.

If the snagged garment is reversible, you can hide the snag more invisibly by using the classic darning method for weaving in ends (page 100).

METHOD: HIDE A SNAG WITH A SNAG REPAIR NEEDLE

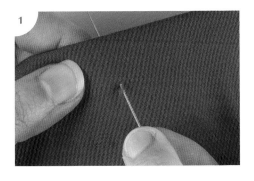

1. Poke the point of the snag repair needle through your fabric, as close as possible to where the snag begins.

2. Grab the needle from the other side and pull it through the rest of the

way, grabbing the snagged thread with it. It doesn't have to pull all of the snag – just enough for you to grab part of it from the other side. Check the other side to see if you have enough to work with; if not, repeat as necessary.

METHOD: HIDE A SNAG WITH A SEWING NEEDLE

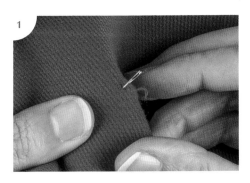

For snag repairs, you poke the needle in first, then thread it. Clever!

1. Poke an unthreaded needle through your fabric, as close as possible to where the snag begins. Push the needle most of the way through, leaving the eye still exposed.

2. Hold the needle on the wrong side of the fabric to secure it, then insert the snagged thread through the eye of the needle. You can fold the end of the snag to create a firmer edge to poke through the eye.

3. Pull the needle the rest of the way through and take the snag with it.

EXTRAS:

shoes

Just like clothes, shoes and slippers made of fabric can be darned, patched and stitched back together when they fall apart (and embellished when they are stained).

Shoes present some additional mending challenges: often they're made of thick materials and the insides are not easily accessible, making hand-stitching awkward. For home shoe repairs, pliers and a thimble are incredibly helpful for moving the needle, and a curved needle can be handy for toes and other tight spots.

Leather shoes can be patched, painted, glued and shampooed (I removed red-wine stains from boots with special leather shampoo). A leather needle is indispensable for stitching leather – it has a sharp, chiselled tip to cut through heavy-duty materials – and heavy-duty thread is recommended. Needle holes poked in leather are permanent; I like to pre-plan my stitch holes when working with leather to avoid regret (as with Leta's dress no. 2, page 228).

Slippers can be resoled with non-skid material when they've worn through – leather or felt work well – and felt slippers can be needle felted back to health.

Separated shoe soles can be reattached with a flexible, waterproof glue like Shoe Goo®. But it's best to leave more complex sole repairs to the professionals and support your local shoe repairer. Unevenly patched or altered soles can affect the way you walk (speaking from experience), and it's not worth risking your comfort, health or safety.

Thank you to menders Kate Brookes, Marlen Meiners and Jared DeSimio for sharing their excellent shoe mends here. ✕

Top left and bottom: Jared DeSimio (U.S.A.) has artistically darned and patched many pairs of shoes.

Middle left: I patched Emma F's sheepskin boots with wool felt on the inside and scrap leather on the outside.

Top right: Kate Brookes (Australia) revived scuffed toes with acrylic metallic paint for leather.

Middle right: Marlen Meiners (Germany) darned and satin-stitched her canvas shoes with embroidery thread/floss.

CASE STUDY: AMANDA'S DRESS

Before

Techniques & materials used

o Hand stitching
o Perle cotton embroidery thread/floss in seven colours
o Chalk pencil for marking sections on fabric

I love embroidery, and it's so useful for mending too. There are a few double-duty stitches that I classify as functional embroidery – straight stitch, backstitch, satin stitch and blanket stitch included – in that they can perform structural duties as well as decorative ones.

Amanda brought this black rayon dress with frayed pockets to the Repair Cafe where I volunteer.

I knew this was a job for satin stitch and my drool-worthy rainbow of cotton perle threads. I used a white chalk pencil to divide each pocket top into sections, and used a different colour thread for each section.

A tip for successful satin stitch is to start and come up through the fabric on the same side of your design each time, and stitch down through the opposite side each time. I used the edges of the seams on the pocket flaps as the guides for my stitches.

After

CASE STUDY: ANNA'S JEANS

Before

o   Patching + hand stitching

o   Denim scrap, salvaged from old jeans

o   Sashiko thread

o   Graph paper and pencil for marking the stitch design

My jeans never get holes in the knees, so I was super excited when Anna commissioned me to mend her favourite pair. She bought them distressed and wanted to keep the ripped look, but the left knee hole was getting too large and bothering her.

I proposed Japanese sashiko stitching and handed her Susan Briscoe's *Ultimate Sashiko Sourcebook* so she could choose the pattern. I was thrilled when she picked the cross pattern – *jujizashi* – because it's one of my favourite shapes to mend (like first-aid for clothes).

Another cool feature of this pattern is that the crosses appear as individual shapes, so you can visually follow the shape of your rip rather than create a solid rectangular pattern block. It's an illusion, though, because – traditionally speaking – the crosses are not sewn how they appear.

Using a grid as your starting point, you stitch all the vertical lines first, then the horizontal ones, so it requires a bit of planning. And it can be tricky if you need to redo or add some stitches – I unpicked and restitched the top four crosses because I wasn't happy with them the first time, and I added a few crosses for extra stability.

I learned so much from this project and noticed my stitches improving midway through. I learned that it looked better if I followed the grid lines rather than try to make the corners meet, which was counterintuitive for me.

→

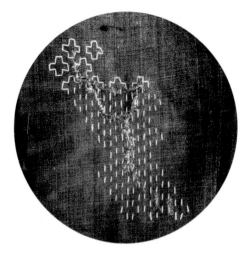

←

Real talk: I'd seen 100+ pairs of sashiko-stitched jeans online before I tried it myself and no one mentioned how hard it is to transfer a grid onto worn-out jeans with rips and colour variations. I stitched these on a weekend away and found that all the fabric-marking pens and pencils I brought with me did not show up on all the shades of denim. Chalk rubs away with sweat, so it's not great for projects with lots of stitching. A yellow disappearing paint pen would have been ideal if such a thing existed but it didn't.

I am stubborn and wanted to finish my stitching on the weekend, so I safety-pinned some graph paper onto the jeans and stitched through the paper, jeans and denim backing patch. It worked, but it took a while to carefully remove the paper when I was finished with the vertical stitches.

I added a few more crosses later in the week for stability – this time I drew a grid of dots on clear water-soluble stabilizer, then pinned it to the jeans. It was a much easier method – brilliant results, and super easy to wash away.

CASE STUDY: AUSTEN'S SHIRT

Techniques & materials used

o   Patching + machine stitching + hand stitching

o   Vintage bias binding

o   Glue stick

o   Sewing thread

I really enjoy the challenge of visibly mending men's clothes, and Austen has some very nice shirts.

This tailored shirt from Hong Kong had a worn-out collar – a common problem. There's a classic mending trick where you unpick a worn collar, flip it over and reattach it so the good fabric is on top and the damaged fabric is hidden underneath. But the trick only works if both sides of the collar look the same. This collar had a complicated reverse side with extra stitching and collar stays, so the trick was useless.

I thought about making a new collar from a different fabric, but I didn't want the shirt to be demoted to party-shirt or gardening-shirt status. Austen sold luxury cars and this needed to be a fancy work shirt.

I patched the worn section with vintage bias binding – temporarily with glue stick first, then permanently with machine stitching, and a bit of hand stitching to tuck the ends in place. The glue stick made it easy to position the binding and get an even curve, and I got a more precise result than I would have if I had pinned it in place.

After

CASE STUDY: BEN'S JACKET

Techniques & materials used

o   Patching + hand stitching

o   All-purpose sewing thread

o   Metallic sewing thread

o   Fusible interfacing and fusible hemming tape

o   Water-soluble stabilizer

Ben, an actor and puppeteer, commissioned me to mend his jacket, which had a long rip. I wanted to embroider over the gash but not conceal it entirely; I suggested lettering and Ben provided the phrase (a line from the play *Peter Pan*).

First I closed the rip: I tucked a strip of fusible interfacing underneath it, between the outer fabric and lining, and carefully ironed it shut. Then it was time for embellishment. I traced the rip onto a piece of water-soluble stabilizer, then traced the letters so they followed the shape of the rip, and pinned it in place.

I chain-stitched the letters with vintage gold sewing thread and quilted all the pieces together, sewing through the lining as well to make it sturdier. The gold thread I used snagged, broke and popped off the needle more frequently than normal embroidery thread/floss or sewing thread, and I had a few battles with the pins in the process (another reason I prefer safety pins for hand mending). If you look carefully on the next page you can see some of my blood on the stabilizer – ouch! – but the end result is worth it.

Once I completed the lettering, I rinsed away the stabilizer. I finished off by stitching with some brown all-purpose sewing thread over the gaps between letters to keep them from fraying further.

When I collected the jacket over a year later to photograph it for this book, I noticed two new rips on the opposite side. I wanted the second mend to be complementary and not compete with the original text. After using interfacing and fusible hemming tape to seal the new rips shut, I stitched over them with brown thread first to make them secure, then added herringbone stitch over the top. I had exactly enough of the same vintage gold thread left over, with about 2cm (¾in) left to spare! The thread had belonged to my friend Kristy's lovely nan who passed away, so I was thrilled to be able to put all of it to good use.

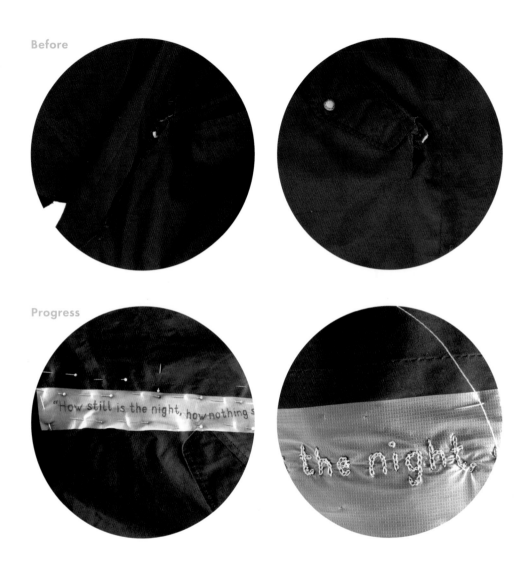

'This is like a second coming for the jacket and it was super rad to see it finished. People have enquired about what the text is, what it means… Sometimes I think people believe it was part of the jacket when I bought it, which is pretty cool.' – *Ben*

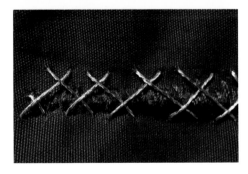

CASE STUDY: CAROLYN'S OVEN MITTS

Techniques & materials used

o   Patching + machine stitching

o   Heat-resistant batting

o   Scrap denim

o   Scraps of cotton bias binding

o   Sewing thread

Carolyn brought these oven mitts to one of the community repair workshops I organized in 2013. They were originally all red, and when I inspected them they were covered in scorch marks and missing large chunks of stuffing, after some culinary adventures.

I had some heat-resistant wadding/batting left over from the time I made a pair of oven mitts, so I knew I could patch up the holes and make the mitts safe to use again. But I couldn't figure out how to make them look good.

Then – in one of my first visible-mending *a-ha* moments – I decided to patch beyond the damaged area and make the mitts look as though they had been dipped in denim.

I filled the holes with new wadding/batting and unpicked most of each side seam so I had flat areas to work with. I patched scrap denim (wrong side out – my favourite side) over the top half of each mitt and sewed over the original quilt lines with my sewing machine.

I sewed on black-and-white bias-binding strips (scraps left over from a different project) to cover the edges. I didn't have enough cross-hatch binding and had to use striped bias binding for one section – a happy accident.

Then I restitched the side seams and turned the mitts right side out – the most difficult part, as the extra fabric layers made the mitts stiffer and the thumbs incredibly difficult to turn out. A smaller seam allowance probably would have made it a bit easier (tip for next time, eh?).

CASE STUDY: CHILLI'S BANDANA

Techniques & materials used

o Patching + machine stitching + hand stitching
o Scrap fabric
o Ribbon
o Fusible web
o Liquid seam sealant
o Sewing thread

Chilli was a darling dog friend and the chief wellness officer at one of my former workplaces. When she ripped her namesake chilli-pepper bandana, I had to help!

I used fusible web and scrap denim to patch the bandana from the reverse and prevent it from ripping further. Then I zigzag-stitched over the rip with my sewing machine to secure all the threads (the red stitching visible in the reverse photo).

The right-angled rip was perfect for a bow. I created the bow in two separate parts: the tails of the bow were stitched on by machine (the teal rectangles visible in the reverse photo), then the loops were added on top and stitched by hand. I used a few drops of liquid seam sealant on the edges of the bow to prevent unravelling.

The bow looked beautiful when I first mended it but was not robust enough for Chilli's active lifestyle. After a year of repeated bursts of joyful doggy rolling it needed a second round of repairs; the fancy notched edges had frayed and the loops had gone floppy. For repair round 2, I trimmed the frayed bow edges and secured them with satin stitch, and hand-stitched the bow loops in place to withstand more rolling around.

I've thought about whether this is visible mending or the opposite – embellishing to hide the mend and keep it a secret. It still makes an impact, regardless – strangers have noticed the bow and commented on its cuteness, which presents ongoing opportunities for Chilli's owner to say it's been mended (if she chooses to). I love inspiring those conversations and showing people that mending doesn't have to be boring or ugly – even for pets.

'Chilli loves going to work. She has become part of a pack and perceives it to be her job to look after her humans throughout the week. One year she was given a chilli bandana as an office Kris Kringle gift and promptly ripped it on a rogue nail the same week. I could have replaced it without great expense but it was a gift from one of her pack, and if she had any attachment to material things I think she'd want to keep her bandana. I repaired it, very roughly considering my dire sewing skills, and Erin offered to improve it. It is a lovely mend that has survived the many upside-down back-scratching sessions that Chilli subjects it to. The best part is walking home through the city every morning and night and, without fail, so many people smile at her jaunty walk and red bandana with the teal bow. It brings a little joy to everyone we walk past – it caused one woman to quite literally stop in her tracks and squeal – which brings joy to Chilli and me.' – *Jac, Chilli's human*

After, front

After, back

CASE STUDY: CLARE'S JACKET

Techniques & materials used

o   Patching + machine stitching + hand stitching
o   Cotton shirting fabric
o   Polyester lining fabric
o   Sewing thread
o   Fabric laminating glue gel
o   Fusible web

Clare commissioned me to mend her much-loved waterproof jacket, which was threadbare and frayed in quite a few spots. The major challenge was that my repairs also needed to be waterproof, so I had to use different methods than I might have otherwise.

First I made bias binding from a striped fabric remnant from the Phillips Shirts factory in Melbourne; the 88 x 70cm (34 x 27½in) piece produced nearly 9.5m (10½yd) of binding. I tested a few different waterproofing methods, including 100% beeswax and a beeswax/coconut oil combination, before settling on a fabric laminating glue gel, which gives fabric the look and feel of oilcloth.

I attached the bias binding to the bottom of the jacket using my sewing machine's walking foot (a lifesaver for thick, heavy-duty layers) and binder/bulldog clips to hold the binding in place without leaving permanent pin holes. The binding looked great but I soon realized that my original plan – to cover all the damage with the binding – was going to be a bit much visually, and I wouldn't be able to cover all the sleeve damage with only one strip of binding. I decided to mix it up with some solid blue patches. I'd discovered that the fabric I'd laminated no longer frayed, so I could experiment with more interesting shapes for the blue patches, made by painting raw-edge fabric scraps with the glue gel.

While the patches dried (a 24-hour process), I made six lining patches using a scrap of lining fabric and the turned-edge appliqué method (page 69) and whip-stitched them in place, being careful not to stitch the lining to the jacket. I turned in each corner with my needle to create a nice sharp point.

→

← Once the blue triangles were dry, I attached them with fusible web (to hold them in place without permanent pin holes) and backstitched them in place. Then I dabbed a small amount of glue gel on the triangle corners with a small paintbrush to secure them.

To finish I stitched bias binding onto the cuffs.

There are 29 patches on this jacket (not including the binding) but six of them are in the lining and 13 are on the insides of the sleeves, so Clare can show them off if she wants to or keep them mostly hidden from view.

CASE STUDY: EMILY W'S JACKET

Before

Techniques & materials used

- o Patching + hand stitching
- o Ribbon
- o Sewing thread

Emily bought this slightly damaged wool jacket at a charity/thrift shop, and asked me to work my magic on the two moth holes close to the bottom front edge.

Emily is a fellow professional wordsmith and happens to have a marvellous surname starting with W – Wrigglesworth – so I couldn't resist the opportunity to create a big W, using the holes as a guide. I'm a typography nerd, so it was fun for me to create a letter by hand from 20cm (8in) of ribbon trim (the minimum you can buy at my local craft store).

I noticed the buttons were a bit loose, so I reattached them with the same turquoise thread, which makes them a bit more special and ties it all together.

Colour inspiration came from my Grandma Bunny, who would have loved this combination and performed her signature peacock bird call in admiration.

Progress

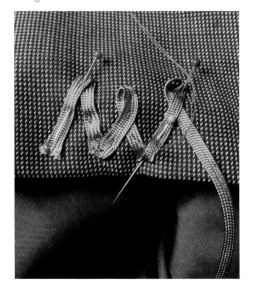

After

CASE STUDY: EMILY O'S DRESS

Techniques & materials used

o   Painting
o   Gold shimmer fabric paint
o   Washi tape

When Emily sent me a photo of this dress – which discoloured when she tried to remove a stain – my first thought was to add a cute pocket over the top. But when I inspected the dress in person, the fabric was thin, delicate and slippery – not what I had imagined and not a great candidate for sewing patches.

My Plan B was to paint gold hexagons over the stain with my sparkly fabric-paint pen. But I discovered that, although the paint pen looks great on cotton, it leaves a weird oily ring on silk and polyester. (Thank goodness I tested it out first.)

Plan C was to apply gold fabric paint with a paintbrush through a stencil made of cardstock. But the stencil tests had uneven edges, so I went with Plan D, which was to tape all the hexagon edges in place.

I found it hard to keep the wriggly fabric straight, so the finished painting was a bit uneven once I removed the tape. The gold paint was fairly easy to work with, though; you could achieve a decent result with it by painting freehand if you're open to a more abstract, free-form design.

Progress

After

CASE STUDY: EMILY O'S SHIRT

Techniques & materials used

o Patching + hand stitching
o A mix of stranded cotton embroidery thread/floss (blue, red, white) and cotton sewing thread (pink)
o Scrap fabric (cotton voile)

Emily commissioned me to mend this gorgeous cotton voile shirt from India, which had ripped along a seam and become threadbare in a few spots.

I knew I'd need to add patches for reinforcement because the fabric was so delicate – too delicate for stitching alone – and the edges of the rip had frayed substantially.

My ideas often change course when I'm working on a commission – you never really know how something is going to look until you try it. I was initially inspired by Indian kantha stitching and wanted to quilt together the shirt and new fabric with parallel lines of running stitch. I didn't love how it turned out, though, and after a few stitch trials (and much unpicking) ended up here. The blue crosses follow the trail of damage and the red, pink and white threads blend in and add strength. The vents in the sleeves were starting to fray, too, so I satin-stitched them closed in pink and added blue crosses to finish it all off.

While I was photographing the shirt for this book, I discovered another frayed area at the front. The good news is that once I've created a mending theme, it's easy to continue what I've started when more mending needs to be done – the creative part is taken care of and I can just get stitching. It's portable, too – I can pack my needle, threads and travel scissors and use up time spent in waiting rooms and on public transport.

My favourite part is how the stitching looks from the inside – the grey cotton voile is the perfect backdrop to display all of the handiwork that went into the repair, and it's so fun and colourful.

'I loved my "hot day" shirt literally to bits... This exquisite, visible, loving and respectful mend by Erin achieves two important things for me: I get to keep wearing this wonderful shirt and it beautifully aligns with the philosophy of the shirt's maker, Anokhi. I purchased this from the Anokhi Museum of Hand Printing shop in Jaipur, India. Anokhi started as a clothing label in Jaipur in 1967. Its founders were inspired by a desire to save the disappearing art of block printing and resurrect a sustainable livelihood for the many craftsmen in and around Jaipur. Anokhi supports artisans to uphold their craft in all their unique ways – a full circle journey for this shirt from the hands of wood-block-printing artisans to our mending artisan-goddess, Erin!' – *Emily O*

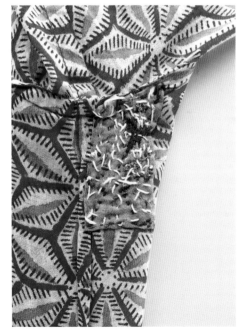

CASE STUDY: EMMA F'S TEA TOWEL

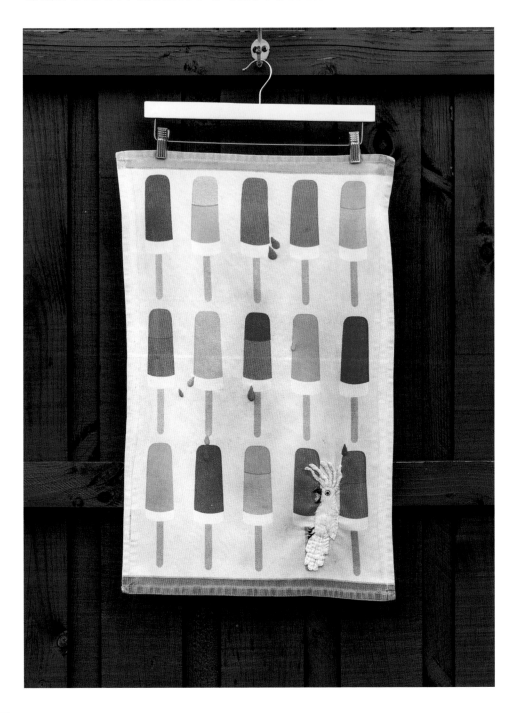

Techniques & materials used

o   Patching + hand stitching

o   Fabric scraps (linen, old sheets)

o   All-purpose sewing thread

o   Stranded cotton embroidery thread/floss in five colours

o   Fusible web

o   Water-soluble fabric marker for drawing drip outlines

Emma commissioned me to mend a hole in this tea towel and I put it off for ages because I only had one idea – the cockatoo – and I wasn't sure how to execute it. I'm the type of person who sees finished art projects in her mind, and the only way to get the images out of my head is to make the things I see.

I loved how the original hole was mostly on the ice lolly/popsicle and immediately knew I wanted to make a cockatoo eating the damaged area, rather than cover it up. I'm a bit smitten by cockatoos, ever since I saw them in a public park when I first came to Australia in 1997. In the USA, they live in cages, but here they roam free! I love their beady eyes and delightfully expressive top knots. I've seen them nibble on everything from houses (apparently they love cedar) to inflatable outdoor movie screens, so ice lollies/popsicles seemed plausible.

My husband, Matt, helped draw the initial concept and I did a bit of free-form patching using fabric scraps in my stash, leaving the edges raw wherever I wanted it to look like feathers.

When the tea towel returned for its *Modern Mending* photo shoot over a year later, I found 10 new spots that needed mending: holes, threadbare areas and stains. I didn't want to make more animals because it would take forever and they would compete with the cocky, the star of the show, for visual interest. So I made drips using embroidery thread/floss and satin stitch. Embroidery thread/floss is inexpensive and readily available in a huge range of colours, so I was able to pop in to my local shop and find perfect colour matches quickly. When new holes appear, it will be easy for Emma to keep adding more drips.

Before

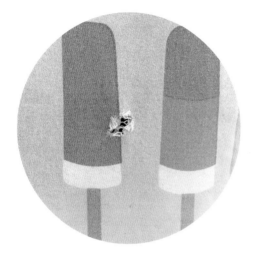

Progress

Back

'I love the guilty
thrill I get from using
art to dry my dishes.'
— *Emma F*

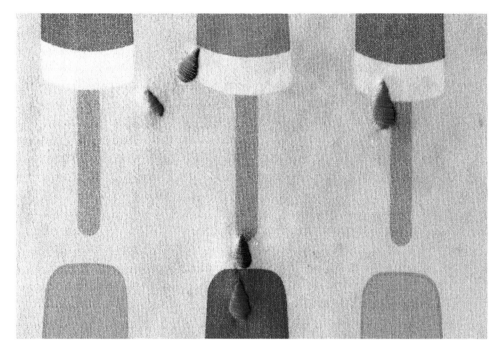

Techniques & materials used

o   Patching + hand stitching + machine darning

o   Stretch denim scraps, salvaged from old jeans

o   Cotton voile fabric scraps

o   Sashiko thread

o   All-purpose sewing thread

o   Liquid seam sealant

o   Fusible web

o   Chalk pencil and air-erasable fabric marker
    for marking design on fabric

Knee holes in jeans are the perfect excuse for sashiko-inspired stitching. As much as I love complicated sashiko stitch patterns, these jeans needed a lot of work and I wanted to try something simpler. The jeans will need to be mended again one day, and a simple design makes it easier for Emma or someone else to continue the theme I've started.

I tried out a few different designs before hitting on the X theme, which ties all the mended sections together.

I made the patches from old jeans – they're stretch denim. They're not perfect rectangles; a simple design meant I didn't have to worry about aligning my grid with imperfect edges.

I added some internal patches – made from cotton voile and fusible web – at stress points to prevent further wear and tear, and darned them in place with a sewing machine and matching thread.

For the sections that weren't damaged enough to require patching, I applied liquid seam sealant to prevent further fraying.

CASE STUDY: ERIN'S SHIRT

Erin, AKA The Rogue Ginger, is a zero-waste queen and stylish lady with a big public profile, so I wanted something a bit sophisticated, not just fun and cute. This is her public-speaking shirt, which she's worn heaps of times since I first mended it. I would love to know how many conversations it's started!

This shirt presented me with a few challenges. It's made of thin, stretchy merino wool (similar to cotton jersey like you'd find in T-shirts), which is trickier than other materials to mend. The kelly-green colour is lovely but did not complement many of the colours I had in my stash of mending materials. And many of my favourite mending supplies for tricky fabrics are not zero-waste – like fusible web, which has disposable backing paper and is essentially plastic-based glue.

I tried needle felting dots over the holes but the fleece didn't stick. So I made felted-wool patches and hand-stitched them in place. Rather than use acrylic felt or buy a whole sheet of wool felt when I only needed a tiny bit, I made my own (see the tutorial on page 134 for instructions): the pink and blue half-circles were needle-felted from wool fleece, and the grey and navy half-circles were made from old, shrunken sweaters that were beyond repair. I used a 3mm (⅛in) diameter coin as my cutting template and split each circle in half before mixing and matching and sewing them on with a tiny running stitch, which blends in to the felt.

→

'I wore this shirt to one of my first major public-speaking events. It was a nerve-racking experience that thankfully went well, so the shirt quickly became my lucky choice for talks. When it developed holes, I was excited because it would become a great example to show off visible mending and talk about it as a way to keep our clothes that little bit longer. Or in my case, to wear for hundreds of talks!' – *Erin*

← As I was getting ready to take photographs of the finished mend, I noticed more tiny holes (of course!). I secured them with tiny cross stitches made of sewing thread, which is easy for Erin to replicate if more holes begin to appear.

Since I first mended this shirt, a few more holes have appeared and Erin accidentally spilled some beeswax on it while teaching a workshop. I added another half circle in peach to cover the long hole on the hem – because I'd used a coin as my template the first time, it was an easy shape to replicate – and new crosses in pale grey over the other holes and beeswax stains.

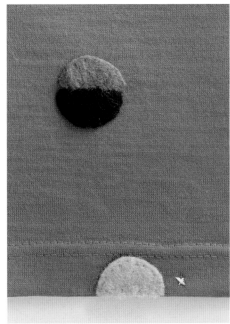

CASE STUDY: GUY'S SWEATER

Before

Techniques & materials used

o Darning + hand stitching
o Stranded cotton embroidery thread/floss in two colours
o Water-soluble stabilizer

Guy is a designer and fellow repair enthusiast. His cotton and silk sweater had a hole in the front and he asked if I could incorporate this red explosion design, a symbol he loves.

Two tools were essential for this mend: water-soluble stabilizer and an embroidery hoop stand, which allowed me to use both hands for stitching. I wouldn't normally use an embroidery hoop for a knitted garment but I was careful not to stretch it too tight, and being able to use both hands was helpful and saved time.

I traced the design onto water-soluble stabilizer and tacked/basted it in place, then backstitched the outline, taking care to ensure the hole was safely within the border.

I darned the hole with navy blue embroidery thread/floss once the outline was complete. Then I filled in the design with satin stitch.

I washed away the stabilizer once I'd finished stitching, which changed the shape of the design slightly so it looks more like a sea monster – a not-unpleasant surprise. The sweater still looks great months later.

Progress

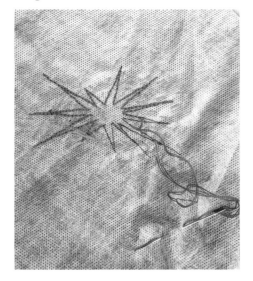

After

CASE STUDY: HILARY'S SHIRT (AKA LARGE MARGE)

o Patching + machine stitching + hand stitching
o Cotton jersey fabric (new and scraps)
o Cotton interlock fabric
o Cotton tape
o All-purpose sewing thread
o Stranded cotton embroidery thread/floss
o Metallic sewing thread
o Fusible web and interfacing

This shirt is the most epic mending commission I have attempted. When Hilary first sent me a photo of it – a sentimental favourite that she admitted was 'held together by optimism only' – I replied: 'Did you get mauled by a tiger?' The neck, bottom band and cuffs all needed new binding and the shirt was riddled with holes.

I affectionately named the shirt 'Large Marge', after a character in the film *Pee-Wee's Big Adventure* who memorably describes 'the worst accident I ever seen'. In my house Marge would have gone straight to the rag box. So why bother mending her? Well, I *hate* it when professional repair people tell me something's not worth saving, and I hoped I might learn something that I could use for teaching purposes.

This was a big job and my sense of 'How the heck am I going to do this?' crept in repeatedly, but I just attacked it bit by bit. Once I had the colour palette sorted, I knew this mend was achievable.

First I overstitched all the edges to reinforce them, keep them from curling and make them easier to re-cover. Then I added arrow patches – made from scraps of cotton jersey and fusible web – to all four side and sleeve seams and backstitched the borders by hand. The arrows stop where the holes stop.

Marge's cuffs were covered in 6cm- (2¼in-) wide strips of cotton jersey that, in another lifetime, were underpants. Yes, underpants! Undies (boxers and briefs) make great rags and patches, and they're usually extra soft from regular washing; just cut off the worn-out sections and re-use the good stuff.

The cuffs feature blocks of colour to make the most of all the odd-sized scraps I had; I machine-stitched them over the original cuffs. I bought new fabric for Marge's bottom band, neckline and shoulders.

→

LESSONS FROM LARGE MARGE

1. Cotton interlock fabric is double-knit so it doesn't curl, which makes it a dream to work with compared to cotton jersey (which loves to curl).

2. You can use strips of cotton interlock/jersey like bias tape (cut straight, though – not on the bias) to cover worn-out edges.

3. That triple straight stitch (|||) on my sewing machine that I'd been ignoring is my friend (hat tip to my friend Kate, who first sang its praises).

4. That triple straight stitch takes at least three times as long to unpick.

5. Do not use cheap, poorly made thread that someone gave you just because it matches. You'll have to unpick it later.

6. All those colourful underwear scraps I saved did indeed come in handy one day.

7. I can mend anything.

8. You can, too! (It's easier if you don't let your clothes get to this point, though.)

9. Mend your clothes as soon as holes appear because you will save heaps of time in the long run, or money if someone else is fixing them for you.

← Confession time: the first time I tried to sew the bottom band, I got the measurements wrong and had to unpick my stitching – for hours – and created a few new tiny holes in the process. Now Marge has triangle patches, or fangs, as I like to think of them, on the back.

The shoulders needed the most work and the most thinking time, so I saved them for last. I patched them from the wrong side with stretchy fusible interfacing, which closed up the curly-edged holes and made everything nice and flat. I used fabric and fusible web to make the red shoulder panels and quilted it all together on the sewing machine, using the presser foot edge as my guide for stitching parallel rows.

Since I first mended Marge, she's busted a new hole in the elbow. So I gave her a special tattoo, using a fabric scrap left over from her first mend and some fancy embroidery.

CASE STUDY: JESS'S SWEATER

Before

216

Techniques & materials used

o   Needle felting + hand stitching

o   Wool fleece in three colours

o   Embroidery thread/floss

When Jess mailed me her favourite dotty wool sweater for repairs, she thought it had a few holes. But I found 19 of them! (They weren't all visible immediately – I had to hold the sweater up to the light and mark it with safety pins first.)

I knew I wanted to mend this sweater with more dots but in a different colour. I prefer needle-felted dots to be the same size – they look more intentional that way – and I wanted to play along with the dots already there. Some of the holes were too large to be covered by just one dot at that size, though, so I got around it by overlapping dots in those areas. I asked Jess to pick two colours for the mend (teal and navy blue) so the overlapping dots would stand out and not look like strange blobs.

When I collected the sweater a year later to photograph it for this book, I found another hole. Then nine more holes. Then three more!

I love mending that tells a story, so I asked Jess to choose a new colour for chapter 2 (ice blue). Jess is a professional teddy-bear maker, and we couldn't resist the opportunity to make one of the new dots a bear. I like that it's a secret polar bear, the same colour and size as the other dots, which makes it more fun.

After

CASE STUDY: KATE'S CARDIGAN

o Needle felting + hand stitching + darning

o Wool and alpaca fleece

o Wool yarn

o Water-erasable marker for tracing the design

o All-purpose sewing thread

When I first mended Kate's cashmere cardigan, it had a hole in the elbow and the cuffs were just starting to unravel.

I needle-felted a large asterisk-shaped patch for the elbow, using a template to make it as precise as possible. To create the template, I cut three thin strips off of an old receipt and fanned them out to make the asterisk shape. I traced the receipt-strip asterisk onto an old envelope and cut it out to make a window (see the bottom-left photo on page 220). I then traced the design onto the sweater with a water-erasable marker.

Because the edges of the elbow hole were a bit scraggly, I used a felting needle to stick them down to the felting surface first – coaxing any curly edges back toward the centre – before adding wool fleece. This ensured my base fabric was flat and not distorted before I mended it – a similar effect to using pins or an embroidery hoop. (A tiny amount of stretching can also be fixed with a steam iron.)

Then I reinforced the cuffs with blanket stitch, using variegated yarn in complementary colours.

While getting ready to photograph the cardigan after its first mend, I discovered another tiny hole on the hip. I patched it with a small pre-felted asterisk in my mending kit (made using the method on page 134, with notches cut into a circle to make the asterisk shape).

Since mending this cardigan the first time, two more holes and a worn spot have popped up. I didn't have yarn or mending wool in the same shade as the cardigan, so I used matching cotton sewing thread to darn the two holes. But I still wanted a fuzzy texture, so I needle-felted over the top with matching alpaca fleece. Only if you look closely can you see the three blended mends.

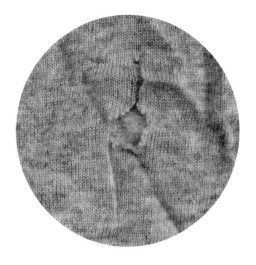
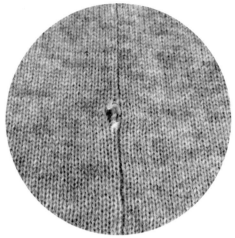

'This is my favourite cardie. I was really sad when I found a hole on the elbow and fraying around the sleeves. I had been following Erin on Instagram and saw some of her mending work, and I knew she'd be the one to save my cardie! I could not be happier – with the beautiful mending work around the elbow and the stitching around the sleeves, it's very much a one-of-a-kind cardie now! Love it and love what Erin does.'
– Kate

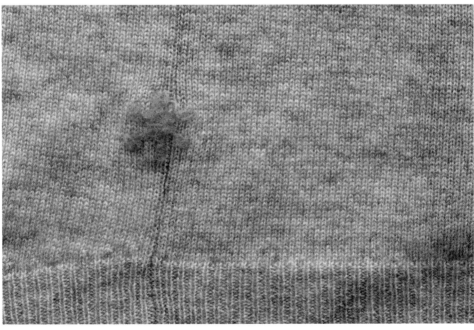

CASE STUDY: KYLIE'S JUMPSUIT

Process

Techniques & materials used

o   Painting
o   Fabric block-printing ink in two colours
o   Masking tape

Kylie commissioned a revamp of her favourite jumpsuit after it had an unfortunate accident at a New Year's Eve party. Legend has it that an overly friendly person who was high as a kite hugged Kylie at the party, and his chemically enhanced sweat bleached her jumpsuit.

When she first told me the story, I thought of embroidering around the stains to make them into a feature. But the fading was too subtle and it was hard to tell where the damage started and ended. So I ended up using fabric block-printing ink and Kylie chose the colours.

This mend terrified me a bit because I had never done anything like it before. The ink is the consistency of toothpaste and I had to buy a mini roller and special paintbrush to apply it evenly. Every colour change took about two days to dry under normal weather conditions, but thankfully we had a 38°C/100°F day and I was able to get through four applications by leaving the jumpsuit outside to dry. (I stuffed the jumpsuit with a pillow to simulate humanity while it dried.) I finished it just in time for party season.

Progress

After

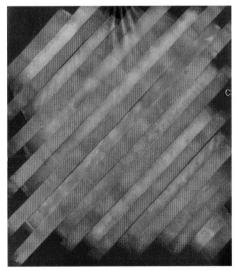

o   Patching + hand stitching

o   Scrap fabric

o   Perle cotton embroidery thread/floss in two colours

o   Metallic sewing thread

o   All-purpose sewing thread

o   Tear-away fabric stabilizer

Leta's beloved cat, Mouska, ripped her dress and she commissioned me to mend it however I liked. Usually I love creative freedom, but I could think of 101 ways to mend this dress and my mind went into overdrive. I decided to *experimend*.

One of my favourite Japanese embroidery books is called *Geometric Flower Garden* (approximate translation; see Recommended Reading on page 264, for details). I use a translation app on my phone to photograph and translate my foreign-language craft books so I can read them, and I was delighted when the app displayed the phrase 'imaginary flowers' (how poetic!) from this book. I decided to make an imaginary apology flower from Mouska. The flower stem is satin stitch and covers the length of the rip.

The petals were created with a sort of punk version of a traditional patchwork method known as EPP (see page 69). I cut the flower shape freehand from scrap paper, folding it up like a paper snowflake first and customizing each section after unfolding. I divided the paper template into six petals and made cardboard templates for each petal – numbering each one so I wouldn't forget how they fit together. I used the cardboard templates to trace and cut the fabric pieces (all scraps from my stash), adding a small seam allowance for each one. I folded in and ironed the edges of each petal with the cardboard template in place. Then I joined all the petals together (as per the original paper template) before stitching them onto the dress with silver metallic sewing thread.

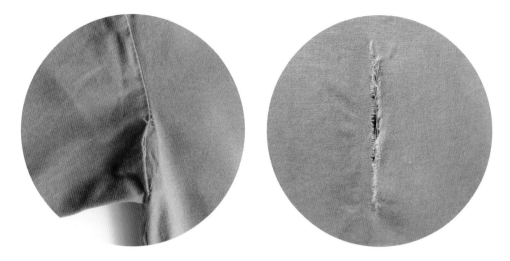

'The apology flower is such a lovely idea. I do volunteer work with refugee kids – they love that flower, and hearing about how it came to be there and what it means. When I'm telling them the story, they always want to see a photo of Mouska, my rescue cat, who was responsible for it in the first place. When Erin sent my dress back, I took photos of Mouska sussing out the apology flower – some people don't think he looks at all sorry. He might look like a wilful creature, but he's actually the most gentle cat I know. I reckon there was just a fault in the fabric and his claw happened to be in the wrong place (which ended up as the right place – thanks, Erin!).' – *Leta*

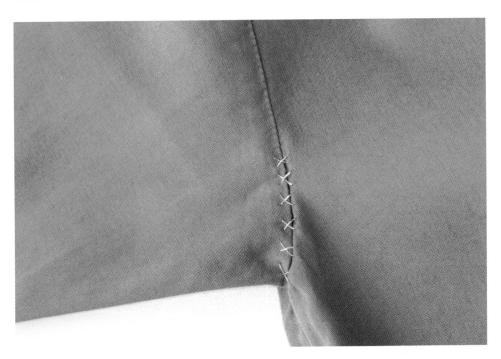

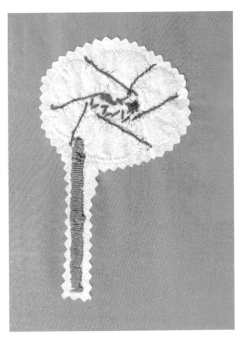

CASE STUDY: LETA'S DRESS NO. 2

Before

Techniques & materials used

o   Patching + hand stitching
o   Scrap of leather
o   Vintage linen embroidery thread/floss

Leta commissioned me to mend another dress after she found a mysterious hole over her right hip.

I love darning linen with a large visible weave, as it provides an easy structure to follow. But I knew from inspecting the damage that something was unusual – the fabric was thinning beyond the hole, which looked like the result of frequent wear and tear, not an accident. After investigating further, we deduced that the cross-body bag she wore every day was the culprit. I knew then that darning would be inadequate and a stronger solution was required – one that could hold up to frequent abrasion.

Taking inspiration from elbow patches, I decided to add a leather patch to the dress. Soon after the idea popped into my head, a student told me about a local leather-jacket factory where she had collected colourful leather offcuts that were otherwise destined for landfill. This scrap was part of a huge bundle pulled out of a factory rubbish bin. I'm vegetarian and seldom use leather, but I hate the thought of wasting it even more, so I was excited to put the scraps to good use.

I soaked, dried and ironed a test scrap of leather to make sure it would hold up OK in the wash. Then I used the scrap to test out different thread colours and stitches.

On the final patch, I poked holes along the border with an awl. Stitching creates permanent holes in leather, unlike fabric, and I wanted to plan out my stitch spacing for maximum consistency.

I finished it all off by stitching it in place with vintage yellow linen embroidery thread/floss, coincidentally a perfect colour match and a nod to the original dress fabric.

After

CASE STUDY: LOUISE'S SWEATER

Before

Techniques & materials used

o   Needle felting

o   Wool fleece in nine colours

When I demonstrated needle felting live on stage a few years ago, I needed holey test subjects to mend, but all of my sweaters had already been mended. Hmmm. So the good people at Sacred Heart charity/thrift shops saved me a few holey sweaters they'd received, like this black wool/angora number, that were otherwise headed for landfill. Win–win!

I was excited about this sweater because it had eight holes scattered around, which meant I could make confetti-like polka dots (one or two dots can look out of place, but multiple dots make it look like there's a cohesive theme).

The back of this sweater (main picture) had all the holes; it's now colourful while the front is all black. My friend Louise is the sweater's new owner; she wears it backwards so the colourful dots are more prominent.

I found one more hole when I photographed the sweater for this book, so I added another dot in a new orange-yellow hue.

Tiny holes can be tricky to locate when it's time to mend them ('Now where was that hole again?'). Black knitwear – and fuzzy black knitwear in this case – is even more difficult because holes blend in and are nearly impossible to see unless you're wearing the garment. To make things easier, I hold items up to the light and use safety pins to mark all the holes before I plan my mends. It allows me to see at a distance how many holes there are and what kind of pattern or design might be possible. I can't tell you how many times I've thought I finished mending something, only to find more holes later. Safety-pinning all the holes before you start can save a lot of time and headaches later on.

Techniques & materials used

o   Hand stitching

o   Stranded cotton embroidery thread/floss in two colours

o   Pen for marking design on fabric

I bought this tea towel for Mandy as a birthday present a few years ago. I really wanted to purchase this particular design for her, but the only one available had a small hole in the fabric.

I am envious of Mandy's drawing talent, so when I gave her the tea towel, I told her I would mend it – if she drew the worm first.

This worm is partly inspired by Slimey the Worm from *Sesame Street*® and was satin-stitched to replicate wriggly earthworm skin. I added one French knot for the worm's eye. The original hole is covered by the black spot where the worm pops out.

I've always loved the design of this tea towel but I reckon we've managed to improve it!

Journalists occasionally ask me how I came up with the idea of the worm. It was such an obvious choice that I don't know what to say – what else could have possibly gone there? It was meant to be.

After

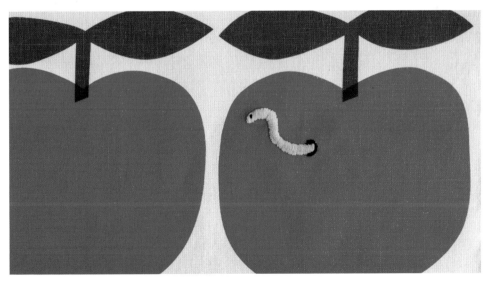

CASE STUDY: MATT'S BOXER SHORTS

Techniques & materials used

o Patching + machine stitching

o Scrap fabric (cotton gingham)

o Sewing thread

These shorts belong to my beloved husband Matt. I used to cut up our holey undies for the rag box and patch pile, but after mending Large Marge (page 212) I started to question whether they genuinely needed to become rags and patches so soon.

Most underwear elastic and thread is not recyclable, compostable or easily reusable (unpicking sewn-in elastic is tedious). Plus boxers often come with plastic buttons, so cutting up undies means a lot of useful but unwanted materials end up stockpiled or in landfill.

I experimended to see if I could make these shorts last longer and still look respectable. I removed a fabric strip around 9 x 60cm (3½ x 23½in) with a ruler and a rotary cutter, then used the strip as a template for a replacement panel, adding extra height for new seams.

I sewed flat-felled seams (enclosed seams that are durable, comfortable and prevent fraying) to join the old and new fabric. Then I tidied up the edges and re-hemmed them.

These shorts have been worn and washed a zillion times since I mended them and they still look good. I've included them here to demonstrate that nearly *anything* is mendable, as long as the undamaged parts of a garment are strong enough for attaching new fabric or yarn.

After

CASE STUDY:
MATT'S PYJAMA TROUSERS

236

Techniques & materials used

o   Darning
o   Stranded cotton embroidery thread/floss (red)
o   Vintage cotton mending yarn (white)

The cat-inflicted hole on Matt's favourite flannel pyjamas had been taunting me for months (see the culprit on pages 45 and 268). Although the hole was small, I knew it would get bigger and more raggedy with every wash and I wanted to stop it in its tracks.

I swear I was guided by colours alone, but I unintentionally made St George's cross – the English flag – with this mend. Each red stripe comprises three rows made from one strand of embroidery thread/floss, and the white yarn is thin vintage mending cotton.

I started to darn this late at night when I was distracted and couldn't quite see what I was doing. I finished the next morning, after some strategic unpicking and reweaving, while wearing my high-tech magnifying glasses with headlight so I could see the details. I took extra care when weaving the red rows, as they are most noticeable.

Although the glasses are fun to have, good lighting is more important to me than magnification. If you're struggling to see your mending, try moving to the best-lit spot in your home (or mending in the sun).

I think this darn turned out perfectly imperfect! It's soft and Matt says he can't feel it at all when he's wearing it, so that's an all-round success.

After

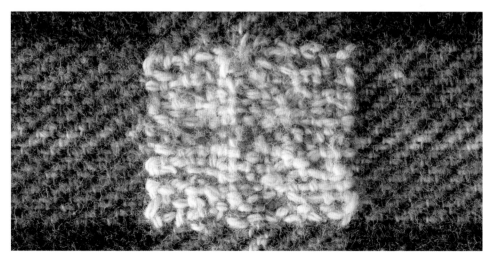

CASE STUDY: NATALIE'S CARDIGAN

Before

Techniques & materials used

o Needle felting + hand stitching + darning
o Wool fleece
o Tapestry wool
o Perle cotton embroidery thread/floss
o Multi-coloured mending wool (a mixture of wool, cashmere, angora and nylon)
o Water-soluble stabilizer

Natalie's wool/silk cardigan had a hole near the neckline.
I needle-felted the hole, then embroidered over the felted dot, using water-soluble stabilizer to stitch the rays without warping the fabric.

Nat's an amazing photographer; the sun is an in-joke about how we met, and a nod to the importance of natural light in photography.

While finishing, I accidentally popped a new hole in the cardie with my embroidery scissors. If you look carefully, you'll see a tiny blended mend, too – I used grey fleece so I wouldn't have to alter my design.

When I collected the cardigan for this photo shoot, I noticed a new hole in the elbow, which I darned with multi-coloured mending wool. It's a subtle mend visually and physically – you can hardly feel it at all. ×

After

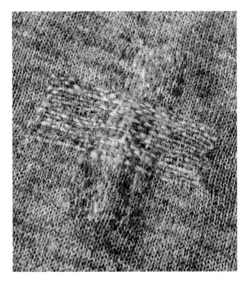

Aleksandra Zdravković / Konfekt Kunststopferei

Hamburg, Germany

Instagram:
@konfekt_kunststopferei_hamburg

**What or who started
you on your mending journey?**
I used to spend summers with my family in my father's little hometown. He comes from a Serbian farming family, and the adults would spend their days repairing all kinds of different things: agricultural tools and machines, water pumps, tyres or sieves.

Mending, though, came from my mother-in-law. She loved designer clothes and would care for and mend her clothes with absolute devotion. She spent her summers knitting, embroidering and mending. It didn't matter if it was inside the house, in front of it, at the river or on the boule course – she was always accompanied by her handicrafts. A lot of those mended gems are, after her passing, still being worn in summer by family members. They are absolute treasures.

In 2016, I started to mend for Räubersachen, a German company that rents out ecological clothes. I still work with them, next to my work for Konfekt.

**Do you have a mending
philosophy or approach?**
Often I look at the holes again and again before I start doing something with them. Sometimes ideas develop over a long time. Other times it's good to follow your first impulse and start while the idea is fresh.

What's your favourite mend so far?
I love repairs for my children because they are always so honestly happy about them. They love to wear their mended clothes.

**What has been your
most challenging mend?**
I've received clothing that just wouldn't talk to me, that I didn't understand. I have learned that it's okay to decline a request for a repair when I get the feeling that we won't work well together.

**What are some of your favourite
mending tools or materials?**
Almost all of my threads are second-hand, as I do not want to consume new resources. I love cashmere, wool, yak hair and silk, but am aware that these products create a lot of harm for animals. Second-hand is the most plausible and least invasive strategy for me. There are already so many nice things there to use!

Favourite place to mend?
Usually it's my desk at work – I keep most of my materials there. But sometimes I prefer to work alone: on my balcony at home, in our kitchen, or in our little allotment garden. There I don't have the big selection of yarns and threads, but I like that – to use what is at hand and make the best of it.

**Can you share a tip or words of
encouragement for new menders?**
Always try to choose a yarn or thread that has the same strength and thickness as the one in the piece you want to mend, and then just go for it. There is nothing like trying it out on your own and figuring it out. Be patient with yourself; it will get better quickly if you keep at it!

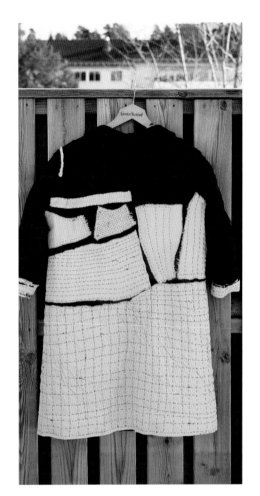

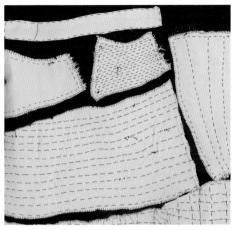

Photographer: Geir Dokken

Eline Medbøe

Oslo, Norway

www.elinem.no

**What or who started
you on your mending journey?**

When I was a kid, my family rented an old house in the countryside that we would vacation in. In the attic we found an old undershirt that had been mended so many times that the original fabric had been replaced. The threads, which were patiently stitched across holes and worn areas, testified to a care and respect for the material and garment. This was made at a time when priority was given to the maintenance of the materials around. The garments were supposed to last a long time and the fabrics were treated for durability so that they could be used again and again. This awareness of materials and maintenance made a strong impression on me and aroused interest in re-use. I was inspired to explore various ways to repair, use, and transform old materials that bear the mark of a story.

**Where do you find
mending inspiration?**

I find inspiration from historical fabrics, art, popular culture. I also find lots of inspiration on Instagram and Pinterest, and through meeting people and holding workshops.

**Do you have a mending
philosophy or approach?**

A good mend clearly shows that someone has used their hands in the process. A good repair imitates life and life is not perfect – that is what makes it so brutally beautiful. Let us highlight the imperfect and human!

**What are some of your favourite
mending tools or materials?**

Linen thread, a long needle and a handmade thimble from leather.

**Do you have a favourite snack / drink
/ music / television show that helps
you mend?**

I love to watch blood-dripping crime series when I'm mending.

Favourite place to mend? On the sofa.

**What's in your
mending pile right now?**

Oh, it's huge! A lot of clothes and jeans from my family and friends. And some old textiles I'm working on for an exhibition.

**Can you share a tip or words of
encouragement for new menders?**

We humans have a great advantage in how our hands are designed. They can be taught to do the finest and most intricate movements. If you are struggling a little at first, keep in mind that it takes some time before your hands learn a new skill. Just keep going, and soon your hands will learn to obey. When I work with materials, I feel that my hands have their own memory and experience. And the more you work with your hands, the bigger the range of experience they get.

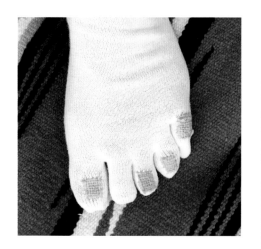

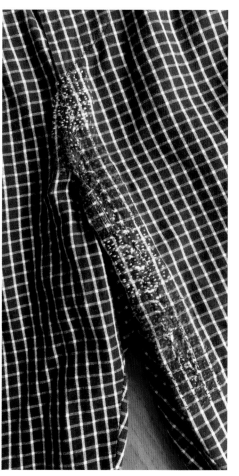

Hikaru Noguchi /
Darning by
HIKARU NOGUCHI

Tokyo, Japan
darning.net + www.hikarunoguchi.com

What or who started you on your mending journey?

I've been running my knitted accessories brand since 1995 and was a bit tired of the fashion industry – creating a new collection every season, which people treat as out of fashion as new trends come and go. And beautiful unused material then becomes industrial rubbish. When I visited Rachael Matthews' yarn shop, Prick Your Finger in East London, she showed me that darning is not about making damaged clothes look new again, but rather repairing them while adding something new. This rescued me from my depression about the unsustainable cycle of the fashion industry.

Where do you find mending inspiration?

Rachael Matthews, Freddie Robins and Celia Pym use traditional darning techniques in inspiring ways. In South Africa, I saw stitched-up workmen's attire with very poor stitch quality but a sense of charm to them. In Tokyo, I see similar things applied to building sites in the city, where things will be covered, sealed off or held together by tape. These small details that surround me are inspiring.

Do you have a mending philosophy or approach?

Mix well. I love using strong colours or different-fibre threads, like cotton thread on cashmere, so it is important for me to choose quality threads, colours and stitches to mix well with the garment.

What's your favourite mending method?

Gomashio darning stitch, which is a sprinkled sesame-seed-type look. This is a really useful stitching method for very light mending through to very heavy mends. It is also very easy, so people who don't have any needlework experience can get quite good results.

Favourite place to mend?

My dining table. I started darning when my children were small and I looked after their homework. I don't need to look after their studies anymore, but I still love to darn at the dining table.

What are your favourite resources for learning new mending skills?

I find interesting techniques from old pieces from museums and vintage shops, like boro, textiles made by poor Japanese farmers which they mended repeatedly to look after their household textiles before the Second World War. I also look at *kintsugi* (a traditional Japanese ceramic-mending skill), as well as any repair and maintenance works (even buildings and cars).

Can you share a handy tip or some words of encouragement for new menders?

Don't wait for the damage to increase or spread. It is easier to start to mend while the damage is not too serious.

Miriam Dym /
Logo Removal Services

Northern California, USA
logoremovalservice.com
Instagram: @logoremoval

**What or who started
you on your mending journey?**
Between 2005–2006, suddenly I became
aware of how much garbage humans
produce. Somehow, I'd managed to stay
blind to this before – garbage is such a
smooth system in the USA, collected then
whisked away, that it's possible to live
multiple lifetimes in ignorance. In 2006,
I started a project to not throw *anything*
out, and to transform all the so-called
garbage my family and I produced into
usable 'new' material.

**Where do you find
mending inspiration?**
I love all the people who take mending to
extremes or make it a big, serious practice.
I also follow a bunch of general repair
people; I love how they do community
outreach and organizing, to make repair
something visible and vital (again). And all
the old-school quilters who work like people
did back in the old days when fabric was
precious – they honour their materials.

**Do you have a mending
philosophy or approach?**
My shop, Logo Removal Services, began as
a way for me to salvage a usable garment,
avoid acting as a billboard, and to add
unusual meaning to something. All of

those things are the philosophy, I suppose.
Celebrate and respect the materials –
the energy and resources, say, that go
into growing cotton and spinning it and
knitting it and the human who sewed it
into a shirt, and poke at and question the
system that makes so much stuff that those
resources are effectively disposable. The
strange shapes, each one unique, worn
where a logo was, provoke questions in
people – a double take is usually required.

**Do you have a favourite snack / drink
/ music / television show that helps
you mend?**
I like quiet when I work. I usually treat
mending and logo-removal activities as
meditation. Unless…

Favourite place to mend?
… if it's as a performance! Live and in public!
I also love to do the laborious hand-stitch
mends during lectures. It helps me with the
annoying problem of having to sit still.

**Can you share a tip or words of
encouragement for new menders?**
When I started Logo Removal, I had
no idea what I was doing. I was lucky to
accidentally discover that cut T-shirts don't
fray! The trick for removal of a logo or
anything from stretchy fabric is to stabilize
it first. I pin new fabric on the wrong side
of the item – that will be in place of the
logo I remove – then stitch it down on
the right side. When it's attached, with
at least two rounds of stitches since I like
the way the thread looks, I trim away the
excess. One thing I love is that when I make
'mistakes', usually because I'm tired, I get
to incorporate them. More stitching! It's all
delightful, if a bit more work.

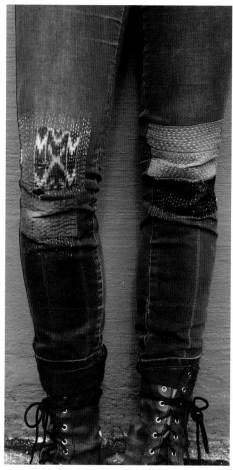

Nina & Sonya Montenegro / The Far Woods

Portland, Oregon, USA

www.thefarwoods.com,
Instagram: @thefarwoods

What or who started you on your mending journey?
Our dad, a carpenter, was very capable of fixing things, but as he is also a puppeteer (and tinkerer), he had his own unique style of repair: relying on wood, wire, glue and red thread, he'd mend busted chairs, the screen door, his belt, eyeglasses, the refrigerator door... Being self-conscious teenagers, we were embarrassed – we couldn't appreciate his ingenuity and uniqueness until much later. Our own mending projects came later as a part of a mission to learn more life skills for resilience, like growing food, preserving, seed saving, foraging, woodworking, etc. We saw learning to repair (and even make our own clothes) as essential skills.

Where do you find mending inspiration?
We stumbled upon artist Michael Swaine and his 'Mending for the People' project early in our mending journey, and have been inspired by his passion for accessibility and fostering community. For years, once a month, Michael parked a cart, outfitted with an old-fashioned treadle sewing machine, on the street in San Francisco and mended clothes local folks brought to him. The mending was helpful, but the real fruit was the conversations and connections the mending instigated.

Do you have a mending philosophy or approach?
We approach mending with a spirit of play – with curiosity, experimentation, and even a bit of reckless abandon. When looking at a pair of jeans with the crotch worn through, we like to ask: 'If I attempt to repair these, what do I have to lose? I already can't wear these, so anything I can do to make them wearable again is a success!' This takes away some of the pressure of perfection and gives us permission to just have fun.

How has your mending style evolved?
We've developed an 'eye' for mending – seeing broken things in a new light – one of excitement and opportunity. As we've practised the basic techniques and added more advanced ones to our repertoire, we've felt more competent and ready to tackle anything and really, we mean anything: straw hats, wicker baskets, shoes, garden hoses, broken teacups, couches... ANYTHING.

What are some of your favourite mending tools or materials?
We have a rather large collection of colourful, unusual materials that we love, so there are lots of good options to pull from when working on a project. We have three stashes: solid-colour and patterned fabric, yarns of all weights and colours, and thread. (Oh, and of course, buttons.)

Can you share a tip or words of encouragement for new menders?
Don't be afraid to mess up. Keep practising sewing – neatness comes with practice and getting more comfortable controlling the needle and thread.

Roberta Cummings

Norfolk, East Anglia, UK

Instagram: @roberta.cummings

**What or who started
you on your mending journey?**

My mum normalized taking care of our
clothing and belongings. Mum's mending
kit at home is in constant use; it lives on the
kitchen counter beside the toaster. When
I left home, I started playing with my new
sewing machine: altering clothes, fearlessly
cutting things up and sewing them back
together again. While on a post-grad course,
Mum came to visit. One evening she was
mending something of mine and attracted
a small crowd of my classmates, who were
fascinated, and she showed a few of us how
to darn. I felt so proud!

**Do you have a mending
philosophy or approach?**

Prevention is absolutely better than
a cure. I try to look after my clothes as
best I can in the first place. Doing things
like hemming trousers to the right length
in the first place so they don't fray; packing
away my woollens in the spring so the
moths don't get to them; and reinforcing
areas that are getting thin before a hole
forms. I see mending as a last resort.
Although I must admit to wearing a
damaged cardigan that has some smallish
holes, with the express intention of making
the holes a little bigger so I can do some
cool darning stitches on them.

**How has your
mending style evolved?**

My hand stitching has gotten neater over
the years. I was never disheartened by my
messy handwork; knowing that I could not
compete with the perfect, even stitching
of my mother was liberating (and I always
thought my wonky stitches were charming),
but improvement is a fortuitous consequence
of practice.

**What's your
favourite mend so far?**

My partner's collection of hand-knitted
socks is an ongoing concern! I got tendonitis
in my forearm a few years ago and had to
stop knitting. It made me sad that all the
socks I'd made for him were wearing out.
So I started with the worst ones and just
had a play. It was a great project for getting
to know my Speedweve darning machine
(pictured opposite, top right) and has really
informed my mending practice since.

**What are some of your favourite
mending tools or materials?**

I love second-hand and collect and use
vintage sewing notions and mending yarns.
My most frequently used tools are my
Speedweve and darning mushrooms.

Favourite place to mend?

An armchair of any sort. I will take my
mending everywhere with me! I'm trying to
orchestrate it so I have a little sewing kit in
the car, in my bag, in the living room.

**Can you share a tip or words of
encouragement for new menders?**

There is no such thing as a bad fix. It is
almost impossible to make it worse! The
goal is to halt damage and if you do that,
however messily, you have been successful!

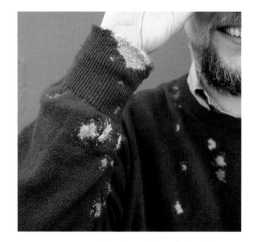

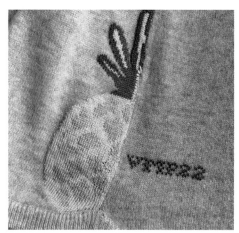

Photo: The New Craftsmen

Tom Van Deijnen /
Tom of Holland

Brighton, UK

tomofholland.com + @tomofholland on
Facebook, Instagram and Twitter

**What or who started you
on your mending journey?**
Ever since I was a teenager, I've been
interested in buying clothes to wear for
multiple seasons (style over fashion).
I have been dabbling with textiles and
needlework since I was a child, so it
just naturally evolved from there. When I
started knitting as an adult and I managed
to make my first pair of socks, I wore
them with much pride, and often; so when
they became my holey socks I started
researching repair techniques, as I wanted
to do as good a job of that as I felt I had
done of knitting them.

**Where do you find
mending inspiration?**
I find inspiration in old darning samplers
and old needlework books. I'm very
interested in techniques, so that drives a lot
of what I do.

**Do you have a mending
philosophy or approach?**
My aim is, particularly when repairing
for others, that the item should be usable
again. I also try to do the best job I can and
understand what my limitations are. That
said, I love a challenge and to do things I've
not done before!

**What's your
favourite mend so far?**
One is a repair on a lovely tailored Jean
Paul Gaultier jacket, where I darned in a
patch using silk threads. I like it so much
because it was a technical challenge and the
lustrous silk contrasts so beautifully with
the wool. Then there's the Six Year Darn
sweater (opposite, top left), just for the
sheer determination of getting it finished!
And I really love the end result.

**What has been your
most challenging mend?**
The Six Year Darn sweater was a
challenge for the enormous amount of
holes I had to fix. The pineapple sweater
repair was challenging because it was
Swiss darning on a teeny-tiny scale,
including repairing an actual hole. But I
seem to learn from every mend I do, even
if it's a technique I've done many times
before; there's always something to try
out and do a bit differently.

**What are some of your favourite
mending tools or materials?**
Darning needles, my thimble and nice
threads made from natural materials.

Favourite place to mend?
At my dining table in front of the window,
so I have good light.

**Can you share a tip or words of
encouragement for new menders?**
Always try to do the best you can and
understand that, like with everything in
life, the more you do it, the more proficient
you will get. ×

CARE: PREVENTION + MAINTENANCE

Mending is marvellous, but having to mend everything all the time is not.
These tips will help you keep your clothes and linens looking their best,
so you won't need to mend as often.

Prevention

Mend early – preventively, if you can – rather than wait for a full-blown hole
or rip to appear.

Use good-quality mending materials, e.g. strong thread for sewing buttons,
so your mends last longer.

Buy well-made clothes. Expensive isn't always better; look for natural fibres
such as cotton, linen and wool, which are easily mendable, and check seams and
buttons to make sure they're sewn properly. Beware of synthetic-blend fabrics;
the synthetic fibres in stretch jeans and leggings often give out after a few years
and cause the fabric to bubble and warp – something for which I haven't yet
found a mending solution. As a rule, the thinner the denim and the higher the
synthetic content, the more quickly they'll wear out. And distressed denim wears
out more quickly than new denim – something to keep in mind if you're thinking
of buying fashionably ripped jeans.

Washing

Before you wash your clothes:

o   Treat stains. Gently spot-clean stains as soon as possible; the longer you
    allow them to set, the harder they are to remove. Avoid rubbing, which can
    discolour clothing permanently. Soaking is a gentler option; soak vintage
    and delicate items only for a minute or two, as dyes can bleed and create
    new stains elsewhere. For oil stains, blot up any liquid by sprinkling it with
    cornstarch or bicarbonate soda, then brush it off and apply liquid detergent
    directly to the stain and let it sit for a few hours before laundering as usual.
    Heat can set stains, so air-drying is best until you know the stain is gone.

o   Zip up any zippers and button their top buttons to keep them closed.
    Unzipped zips can catch on other clothing, causing snags and rips.

o   Empty your pockets. Tissues and lip balm can wreak havoc in a wash cycle.

o   Turn clothes inside-out to prevent fading and pilling.

o   Place delicate items into a mesh laundry bag before machine washing.

Everyday lightly soiled items can be washed in cold water, which saves energy
and is gentler to clothes.

When washing woollens or delicates, use wool wash or a mild detergent. If the care label on your woollen clothing says it's safe to wash in the washing machine, use a gentle cycle (hand-wash or delicate) if your machine has one.

Wash clothes only if they really need it, not after every wear. Spot cleaning and airing clothes will help them last longer (and save water and energy). Spot cleaning is great for most fibres, but soaking is better for silks, rayon and Tencel, where spot cleaning might leave a water mark.

Drying

Air-drying clothes on a line or rack uses less energy than a clothes dryer. I prefer the smell of line-dried linens, too. I love playing 'rain chicken' – I have a rain-alert app on my phone that warns me when rain is coming, so I can keep clothes on the line for longer (and snooze on the sofa in the meantime).

The sun is a powerful disinfectant and whitener. Hang wet clothes inside-out to prevent fading or right side out for brighter whites. I usually dry black and delicate clothes on a clothes rack in the shade.

Dry sweaters and other knitwear flat on a clothes or towel rack, as hanging will distort their shape and a clothes dryer will cause shrinkage. When the clothes are partially dry, you can gently reshape them with your hands.

Storage

Wash woollen clothes and blankets before storing to prevent moth attacks. Moths love dirt and human smells but hate cedar, lavender, cloves, rosemary and thyme; make scented sachets to repel moths. For an active moth problem, put fabric items in your freezer for two weeks to kill moth eggs or larvae.

Maintenance

o **Liquid seam sealant** seals frayed edges and prevents further damage. It's particularly useful for extending the life of jeans on pocket edges and hems.

o **A fabric comb (sweater comb)** removes pilling from fuzzy knitwear and is particularly effective on cashmere.

o **Clothes dye** can revive faded clothing. There are different dyes for natural and synthetic fibres; follow the dye manufacturer's recommendations if your garment contains both. Dyeing stained clothing is a bit hit and miss; sometimes the dyed garment looks brand new, and sometimes it just looks darker (or a different hue) but you can still see the original marks you were trying to hide in the first place.

SHARE THE LOVE + INCREASE YOUR IMPACT

My wish for this book is to share my love of mending with you and to give you the knowledge, enthusiasm and confidence to mend just about anything. Mendy problem-solving is such a fantastic skill to have; why not share what you've learned with others and lower your environmental impact?

I was mending long before I became environmentally conscious; it was something I did in isolation without really thinking about it. But now there is an international community of people who are more environmentally aware and keen to revive the art of mending, and you can help that community grow.

Mending can be a powerful act; sharing your love of mending with others even more so. If you'd like to make the most of your mending and increase your impact, here are a few suggestions.

Start conversations

o **Wear visibly mended clothes proudly.** Visible mending is a great conversation starter, and a visibly mended garment is the perfect uniform for the reluctant activist because it does the heavy lifting for you. Whenever you wear something visibly mended and chat with someone about it, you're raising awareness that mending is possible, it can be creative and colourful, and caring for our clothes is an important thing to do. (When I tell people I'm a professional clothes mender I get a lot of polite nods. But when I show them examples of my mending, they perk up and get excited. Sometimes you need to see it to get it.)

o **Mend in public.** To inspire even more conversations, try visible visible mending – mending in public! The act of mending in public is interesting and unusual, which has the potential to spark conversations and make mending seem more mainstream and possible. Take your mending with you when you travel, on your lunch break or when you know you'll be waiting around somewhere like a doctor's office. (I like to plan my mends, choose colours and do any fabric-marking and pinning at home, then save my hand-stitching and darning – which are repetitive and time-consuming – for mending on the go.) Keeping a simple mending kit at work might spark a conversation or two with work colleagues and show them it's easier than they thought.

Share your knowledge

o **Teach a friend to mend.** The next time you notice a hole or missing button on a friend's clothes, ask if they'd like you to teach them how to mend it. Or if you have children in your life, teach them how to mend their own clothes rather than doing it for them. (I started using a sewing machine at the age of nine and have taught children as young as four how to sew. The four-year-old had the best time and did a brilliant job; the older you get, the more self-doubt and perfectionism you have to wade through.) If you're not sure how best to mend something, you can read this book together and learn on the job.

o **Teach a workshop.** Once you have a few mends under your belt, you could begin teaching others what you know. You don't need to be an expert to teach others. *Repeat after me: You don't need to be an expert to teach others.* (And what makes someone a mending expert, anyway?) Even if your experience was limited to sewing on buttons, you could still offer to teach your work colleagues how to sew on their buttons. You'd be surprised by how many people don't know this skill already and are willing to learn.

o **Volunteer your mending skills.** Volunteering at a repair event is a fun way to give back to your local community and get more mending practice. At the time of writing, there are more than more than 2,000 Repair Cafes and repair initiatives worldwide. If you don't have a repair initiative in your community, you can always start one – repaircafe.org has a starter kit available for download. You don't need to have mending skills to volunteer, either; community repair organizers need greeters, photographers, social-media stars and general helpers, too.

Share your toys

o **Swap before you shop.** Offer to swap fabric scraps and threads with other mendy friends to refresh your stash of supplies and keep things interesting. Sometimes I get tired of looking at the same fabric scraps that I know I'll never use, but someone else might love them. You could start a scrap library with your friends (maybe it lives in a small suitcase?) so you all have access to supplies when you need them, but each of you doesn't need to purchase everything. Or organize a 'restash' event in your community so everyone can trade the fabric scraps, threads and tools they no longer find useful with things they do. You'll save items from landfill and get inspiring new supplies (and conversations) for free!

o **Make mending kits for others.** Do you know someone who'd like to mend but wouldn't know where to begin, or they're time-poor and can't easily access mending supplies? Put together a simple mending kit in a jar or cake tin and offer to help them get started with a lesson or two (or this book).

→

o   **Share this book.** When you're finished with this book, pass it on to someone else who might be able to use it. And ask your local library to purchase mending books (see Recommended Reading on page 264 for my favourites) so they're available to the wider community for free.

Get social

o   **Share your mending on social media.** Like mending in public, sharing your mends on social media helps to raise awareness and make mending more mainstream. The more often you share your mends, the more likely your friends are to start asking you about them and requesting your assistance to get started. You can use the hashtag #visiblemending to inspire others outside your social network. I run a friendly Facebook group called Modern Mending Club where people can get advice and mend-spiration; connecting with others helps increase our sense of community and boosts mending confidence.

Tip: people love a good makeover reveal, so try to take 'before' photos of your mending projects to show the extent of the damage. If someone else has the same problem (e.g. a hole in the elbow of a sleeve), they're more likely to try to solve their problem, too, because they can see the transformation and how it could be achieved.

o   **Host a mending bee.** Mending bees can be fun, and they provide extra motivation to attack your mending pile while catching up with friends. Those who have a bit more experience can share their knowledge, and everyone gets inspired by seeing what others are mending. I've hosted mending bees in my home and provided tea, snacks, good music, mending books and the use of my sewing machine; each time I've received a deluge of thank-you notes and my friends have begged me to host another one. For your mending bee you could invite just your friends (and potentially friends of friends), or you could start a social mending group in your community and make new friends, too.

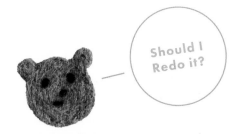

Should I Redo it?

You might squint at your mending at some point and ask yourself 'Should I redo it?', or 'Is it finished?' Here's another question: will it bother you when you wear it? If not, you're done and there's no need to worry.

Even the most experienced menders make imperfect stitches. Sometimes the mend I imagine in my mind is quite different to the mend I make and I reconsider my choice of colours and fabrics, and sometimes even my sanity. What was I thinking? Am I ruining this shirt? Will the shirt's owner like it? It's similar to stage fright and it happens to the best of us; don't let it prevent you from trying, because *it's in the trying that we learn and improve*, which gives us more confidence for the next mend.

Perfection is unlikely, even if you take your time, so it's best not to aim for it. Try 'better than new' or 'wearable' instead. But if you're wondering whether it's possible to redo your mending, here's a basic guide.

Stitching and darning

These are sturdy techniques and will stay intact with regular machine washing. You can usually unpick stitches and redo them easily.

If you're mending fine, delicate fabrics, it's possible to unintentionally make permanent holes or pull threads in the fabric with your needle. A thinner needle and thread are recommended when mending delicate fabrics to minimize any potential damage.

If you unpick tiny machine stitches or stitches that blend in with your fabric and are hard to see, it's possible to damage your fabric in the process. It's better to use a medium stitch length in case you need to unpick it later.

If you're mending leather or vinyl, stitching can be removed but note that needle holes will be permanent.

Patching with fusible web

This is technically permanent, although if you are sneaky and careful you might be able to iron over the patch to melt the glue and quickly remove it (while wearing gloves so you don't burn yourself). The fabric that you patched will have glue residue that you can't remove, but you will be able to put another patch in its place.

Patching with glue stick

This is temporary and the glue will wash out in a regular machine cycle, although you don't want to be too heavy-handed with the glue because it might leave residue where you don't want it.

Needle felting

It's semi-permanent. The more you felt the harder it is to remove, but if you are careful and lift one or two fibres at a time, you can usually pry off a felted patch. Once it's fully felted it will stay intact, provided you wash your woollen garments by hand or on a delicate cycle. (The exception is socks; regular wear can rub away a felted patch so needle felting is not recommended for socks.)

MENDING FOR OTHERS
+ VALUING YOUR TIME

Mending for others can be a lovely way to show you care – about the planet and the people you love. When you mend for others, you're giving them your time, energy, creativity, knowledge and experience.

Well-loved clothes wear out, and there will always be mending opportunities among your friends, family and community if you want them.

You don't have to charge money for your services like I do – you could barter or your mending could be offered as a gift. Whether you decide to go pro or offer your mending services freely, the following considerations should help you establish a value for your time, energy and expertise.

Nobody knows how long it will really take you to mend something (not even you).
Every mending project is unique, which makes it difficult to estimate the time required, especially if it's a creative mend. I often spend longer planning colours and designs when I'm mending for others. Factor in extra time if you need to source mending supplies, and time for taking before-and-after photos.

Surprise! There are always more holes.
I always seem to find more holes or rips than discussed; often the client isn't even aware of the additional damage. Extra holes can add time to a project, and affect the design if you've carefully planned a pattern or colour palette.

One option: set a price for the number of known holes and ask the owner whether to ignore additional holes, or mend and charge more. Or ask them to place a safety pin on every spot to be mended – everything else will be left as is.

I usually charge clients a flat fee, calculated with an hourly or daily rate in mind, plus the cost of any new tools or materials I need to purchase. If you want to charge someone less than full value because you think a fair price sounds expensive and will discourage them, I encourage you to ensure you're getting some other benefit from the project to boost its overall value.

Occasionally I'll quote a price of 'pay what you feel it's worth'. Sometimes this confuses people because we're not accustomed to paying for things this way. And fast fashion can be acquired so cheaply now that a $10 T-shirt – created using 2,700 litres (713 US gallons) of water and made by farmers who grew and picked the cotton, people who processed and dyed the cotton, workers who created the fabric, drivers who delivered it to the factory, pattern cutters and sewists – starts to seem normal, and paying someone more than $10 for their time and materials to mend it seems weird. Which is even weirder when you think about it. Just because fast-fashion prices are bonkers doesn't mean you have to accept less money for your time.

Handle with care.

It's a nice idea to provide washing instructions with a garment you've mended, e.g. 'hand-wash only' or 'wash/iron inside-out'. This can prolong the life of the item and ensure your work is always looking its best. Sometimes I provide extra patches or yarn, too, to make it easier for the owner to mend the item in future.

It's okay to say no.

You don't have to take on anyone's eco-guilt because you can't or don't want to honour their mending request. When I volunteer at my local Repair Cafe, I like to teach people how to mend but I don't usually do the repairs myself; I can make more of an impact in less time by sharing my skills.

 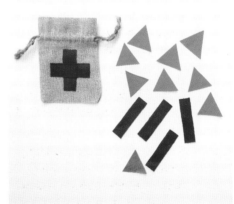

Two 'first-aid kits', given to Hilary and Emily when I returned their mended shirts

RESOURCES: WHERE TO FIND MENDING SUPPLIES

Before you shop

I hope that my evil plan has worked and you can't wait to go on a 'mender bender', as my friend Kat would say. But before you head off on a shopping spree, I encourage you to make the most of what's around you first.

Shopping for anything new has an impact on the planet, if you factor in the raw materials, water, energy, packaging and transport used to make it. If the name of the game is to love the stuff we already have, that includes the clothes we own *and* the tools and materials we use to mend them.

Try these tips and you might find everything you need in other ways:

o   **Use what you have!** Love what you have! This is the most environmentally friendly option and beats other factors like recycled, organic, ethical, etc. Having fewer choices can be more creatively inspiring, and visible mending is a chance to embrace new colour combinations.
    Tip: if you store your supplies in one place, you can see more easily what you have and what might be missing from your kit.

o   **Ask friends and family for what you need.** You might be surprised by what you can find within your network. People who sew and knit usually have more fabric, yarn scraps and needles than they could ever use; they will be thrilled to 'destash' and to know you're putting their leftovers to good use.

o   **Support your local charity/thrift shop.** I love a good charity/thrift shop rummage! My favourite ones have a dedicated section for crafty bits and pieces that could be useful for mending. If your local charity/thrift shop doesn't have a dedicated sewing section, tell the staff what you're looking for and they might keep an eye out for you.
    Tip: if you volunteer at a charity/thrift shop, you get first dibs on the best mending supplies (and beautiful cashmere sweaters in need of mending!) and help your community at the same time.

o   **Search for second-hand supplies online.** Local sharing networks (e.g. Facebook buy/sell/swap groups and Good Karma groups) are perfect places to request what you need, and you get to meet nice neighbours. Etsy, eBay and Gumtree are good sites to hunt for specific second-hand items like embroidery thread/floss, mending wool and darning mushrooms.

USA

Modern Mending shop (modernmending.com) – my favourite mending supplies in one place

Purl Soho (purlsoho.com) – for stitching and darning supplies, including crewel wool

Fabscrap, NYC (fabscrap.org/shop) – for designer fabrics and trims that have been diverted from landfill

Miniature Rhino (miniaturerhino.com) – for sashiko-inspired stitching supplies

Snuggly Monkey Crafts (snugglymonkey.com) – great for premium stitching, patching and darning supplies

Sarafina Fiber Art (sarafinafiberart.com) – for wool fleece and needle-felting supplies, including burlap felting pillows

The Woolery (woolery.com) — for needle-felting supplies

Big Sky Fiber Arts (bigskyfiberarts.com) — for wool and other animal fleeces (alpaca, yak, camel) and needle-felting supplies

Living Felt (livingfelt.com) — for wool fleece and needle-felting supplies, including needle-felting foam made from soy

Peace Fleece (peacefleece.com) — for ethically produced wool/mohair fleece in fabulous colourways

UK

Modern Mending shop (modernmending.com) – my favourite mending supplies in one place

The Village Haberdashery (thevillagehaberdashery.co.uk) – huge range of supplies for your mending, from stitching, patching, darning, needle felting supplies and even jeans thread for machine darning and darning feet for sewing machines

Loop (loopknittingshop.com) – for lovely embroidery and darning supplies

Beyond Measure (shopbeyondmeasure.co.uk) – for lovely embroidery and darning supplies

MacCulloch & Wallis (macculloch-wallis.co.uk) – for sewing supplies, including eco-friendly threads

Wild and Woolly (wildandwoollyshop.co.uk) – knitting yarn for darning, with a section for second-hand bargains

World of Wool (worldofwool.co.uk) — for a huge range of wool, vegan and alternative fleeces

263

RECOMMENDED READING

For out-of-print books, try your local library; you can also visit worldcat.org to search all the libraries where particular books are held. Other spots to search for out-of-print books are eBay, abebooks.com and bookfinder.com.

For Japanese books, Japanese book retailer Kinokuniya has an English-language online shop: united-states.kinokuniya.com. Etsy and eBay are other good online resources for Japanese craft books.

I use a translation app on my phone to decipher my foreign-language DIY books. If it's a translation I'll want to refer to in future, I write down the translation on a separate piece of paper and clip it to the page for next time. I use a translation app on my computer, too, to order the books I can't get through English-language booksellers (one of my secret thrills).

Mending books

Darning Repair Make Mend
by Hikaru Noguchi
A modern, colourful celebration of darning, with gorgeous examples covering a range of applications. It's an essential part of my teaching kit.

Lappa (Patch) and *Stoppa (Darn)*
by Katarina Brieditis and Katarina Evans
Swedish-language mending guides featuring stunning photographs and plenty of technical illustrations so you don't need to understand Swedish to find them worthwhile. Recommended for colour lovers and an essential part of my teaching kit.

Little Fixes: 54 Clever Ways to Extend the Life of Kids' Clothes by Disney Powless
A fun book with instructions for mending and altering kids' clothes to make them last longer.

Make + Mend by Jessica Marquez
An excellent, modern sashiko primer with thorough instructions for prepping and marking fabric before mending.

Make Do and Mend: Keeping Family and Home Afloat on War Rations – Reproductions of Official Second World War Instruction Leaflets, foreword by Jill Norman
A fantastic resource and time capsule with wonderful illustrations and mending tips from 1943. There are two books called *Make Do and Mend* based on the same information, but I prefer this version, with full brochure reprints and the foreword by Jill Norman.

Mend! A Refashioning Manual and Manifesto by Kate Sekules
This fun book includes a fascinating history of mending and a deep dive into different fabrics and mending materials.

Mend It! A Complete Guide to Clothes Repair by Maureen Goldsworthy (1979, out of print)

My go-to resource when I need to research traditional techniques, this is the book to seek out if you're interested in advanced invisible-mending methods.

Mending Life: A Handbook for Repairing Clothes and Hearts by Nina and Sonya Montenegro

A beautifully illustrated book with helpful diagrams (including side views of stitch methods) and lovely stories.

Practical Home Mending Made Easy by Mary Brooks Picken (1946, out of print)

A comprehensive classic mending resource, this book has superb illustrated diagrams for many mending methods, and a dose of antiquated history with reference to women's place in society.

Thrift with a Needle: the Complete Book of Mending by Mildred Graves Ryan (1954, out of print)

Another great classic resource, with a variety of techniques and dainty diagrams. Hard copies are scarce but a digital version is free to view at hathitrust.org.

....

Other useful books

A Dictionary of Color Combinations by Sanzo Wada, published by Seigensha

This is my favourite book for colour inspiration when I'm feeling indecisive. Based on a six-volume Japanese work from the 1930s, it features 348 stunning colour combinations.

Alison Glass Appliqué: The Essential Guide to Modern Appliqué by Alison Glass

A colourful, modern look at making decorative patches, using a few different techniques and finishing methods.

All Points Patchwork: English Paper Piecing Beyond the Hexagon for Quilts and Small Projects by Diane Gilleland

The best resource I've found on the English paper piecing (EPP) patchwork-quilting technique, which you can use as a springboard for making geometric patches for mending. It's thoughtful and thorough.

Boro: Rags and Tatters from the Far North of Japan by Yukiko Koide and Kyoichi Tsuzuki

A historical reference book in Japanese and English featuring beautiful stories and photographs of traditionally mended boro textiles. I love this book but it can be difficult to purchase outside Japan; try Kinokuniya's online shop.

Colour Confident Stitching by Karen Barbé

A beautiful book with inspiration for colour combinations, and design inspiration for surface darning and embroidery.

Crafting with Cat Hair: Cute Handicrafts to Make with Your Cat by Kaori Tsutaya

A fun and unusual resource with clear instructions for using cat fur for felting projects, including needle felting.

Embroidery on Knitting: Inspirational Modern Designs for Stitching onto Knitted Garments by Britt-Marie Christofferson

Visual inspiration for embellishing your mends to make them extra-special. This book has a colour palette that makes my heart sing!

Fashion Revolution fanzines:

No. 001: Money Fashion Power

No. 002: Loved Clothes Last

No. 003: Fashion Environment Change

No. 004: Fashion Craft Revolution

These zines are great for learning more about fashion ethics: how our clothes are made, the wastefulness of the fashion industry, and what we can do to make our clothes last longer. →

←

Field Guide to Stains by Virginia M. Friedman, Melissa Wagner and Nancy Armstrong

A useful stain-removal resource with colour photographs and fun descriptions.

Geometric Flower Garden (approximate translation) by Tomoka Taka, (ISBN 978457911505)

This Japanese book has no English translation, but it's one of the most colourful, inspiring and well-loved embroidery books in my collection and a popular one with my students. It's worth seeking out for the photographs alone.

Hirameki: Cats & Dogs by Peng and Hu

Fun inspiration for turning clothing stains into works of art. The authors transform watercolour paint splotches into animals with black ink, which could easily be replicated with black embroidery thread/floss.

México Bordado by Gimena Romero

A Spanish-language embroidery book with no English translation, this book features plenty of colourful visual inspiration in a number of different embroidery styles. It's worth seeking out for the pictures alone.

Needle Weaving Techniques for Hand Embroidery by Hazel Blomkamp

A good source of surface-darning (needle-weaving) inspiration if you'd like to try more complex weaving patterns.

Organic Embroidery by Meredith Woolnough

If you enjoy machine darning, this is a colourful, well-written glimpse into the world of possibilities with free-motion stitching.

Painting With Wool by Dani Ives

This book will take your needle felting to the next level, with clear instructions for mixing colours and making complex shapes and designs. There's also a fantastic e-course at www.daniives.com.

Simply Stitched with Appliqué and *Zakka Embroidery* by Yumiko Higuchi

I love Yumiko's embroidery style and her books. *Zakka Embroidery* is embroidery only and *Simply Stitched with Appliqué* combines it with patching.

Slow Clothing by Jane Milburn

A slow-fashion manifesto with tips for the thoughtful purchasing, wearing and upcycling of clothes.

Stainless by Shannon Lush and Trent Hayes

A handy stain-removal resource for clothing and other household objects.

Sublime Stitching by Jenny Hart

An excellent, modern embroidery primer with iron-on transfers.

The Art of Frugal Hedonism by Annie Raser-Rowland with Adam Grubb

A hilarious, inspirational resource for living with less stuff and having a joyful life. I have recommended and loaned out this book so many times I've lost count. Don't let the serious cover fool you; it made me snort-laugh from beginning to end.

The Geometry of Hand-Sewing by Natalie Chanin

A gorgeous stitch resource, this book shows the front and back of each stitch pattern, has right-handed and left-handed diagrams and two handy plastic grid templates for marking fabric.

The Sewing Bible for Clothes Alterations by Judith Turner

Instructions for adjusting the fit and style of your clothes to get more wear out of them, along with handy tips for zipper replacement.

The Ultimate Sashiko Sourcebook by Susan Briscoe

The best English-language guide I've found to sashiko stitching, with a comprehensive stitch-design library. ✕

ACKNOWLEDGEMENTS

Thank you:

- to Matt, my favourite human, for all the meals, pep talks, cat wrangling and endless cups of tea, and for helping me turn our home into a photo studio.

- to my mending students, for your enthusiasm, thoughtful questions and for teaching me as much as I taught you.

- to my mending clients, for patiently trusting me with your treasured textiles and allowing me to experimend.

- to my fellow modern menders Eline, Hikaru, Miriam, Nina, Roberta, Sonya, Tom and Zaki – for inspiring all of us to mend more beautifully.

- to my dream team Coco, Emily and Claire, for believing in this book and for turning my wild ideas into awesomeness.

- to my tutorial readers Mary Ellen, Kate, Collette, Agy, Geraldine and Kelly for your insightful editing suggestions.

- to Sheralynn and Kate, for saving the day and enthusiastically stitching and knitting sample swatches.

- to Amy, June and Jacob at the Sacred Heart Mission charity/thrift shops in Fitzroy North, Elsternwick and Preston, for squirrelling away a secret stash of clothes in need of mending (some of which are featured in this book).

- to everyone who donated their photogenically damaged zippers, jeans, socks and tea towels.

- to Natalie, for helping me update my photography and photo-editing skills for the 21st century.

- to Ramona, for your excellent tips on making a book and managing life while doing it.

- to Madeleine, for hosting the fantastic Side Project Sessions (sideprojectsessions.com) where much of this book was written.

- to Hilary, for your lovely words and continuing support.

- and to Miko, World's Best Cat 2002–2018, and Chilli, bandana model and office dog extraordinaire, who passed away while this book was in production.

ABOUT THE AUTHOR

Erin Lewis-Fitzgerald is Australia's leading clothes-mending practitioner. Her mending has been displayed in art exhibitions in Melbourne and Adelaide and she teaches workshops across Australia.

Erin began her career in journalism at the age of 15, and over two decades worked as an editor, sub-editor, writer, and photographer – all skills that came in handy for her first book, *Modern Mending*. After leaving journalism, she founded Bright Sparks, a social enterprise that repaired and re-used electrical appliances to keep them out of landfill.

When she's not trying to save the planet stylishly, you can find her making tiny dioramas for her magic letterbox or cooking up a storm for her cookbook club, the Ottolenghi Appreciation Society. Her retirement dream is to run a deluxe hospital for stuffed toys.

You can find her online at erinlewisfitzgerald.com and modernmending.com.

INDEX